Pink Zebra

PUBLISHING

The
Anti Self-Help
Book

Alice Frick

Pink Zebra
PUBLISHING
Pink Zebra Publishing

Pink Zebra
PUBLISHING

I am dedicating this book to _____.

(please insert the name of a nice person)

ACKNOWLEDGEMENTS

A massive thank you to Nat Sattavet Charusingha for joining me on the journey of creating this book and for his artistic brain that made every graphic better and funnier than I could have imagined. Nat is not only great to work with, but also a friend I will always be thankful for. He is the kind of person who understands me before I understand myself.

I also want to thank Kirsty H. who devoted many hours of her time in dealing with my poetic English – turning sausage roles into sausage rolls, making a dessert a desert and her endless patience with me for spelling Ryanair wrong, yet again. She's spent too much of her life in never-ending online calls with me, reading over and working through all the chapters of this book.

Many thanks also go to Dr Hebba Haddad, who joined me on this fun but intensive journey and received endless research text messages from me, asking things like: "Do people from drug cartels have tattoos?". She was able to answer most of my questions but, even now, I'm too scared to ask her how she got all this knowledge.

And a massive thank you to Sarah Tempest, a very supportive and constructive editor and proofreader, who not only word-polished chapter by chapter but also led me through the final obstacles before publishing.

Last but not least, I want to thank my family starting with my grandparents for being great grandparents and my sister Julia, who set an example in writing when we were children. I copied her in writing stories instead of doing my homework and she has always been a great supporter of my work (not my homework, though).

I also want to thank my parents who have constantly supported me and my creative endeavours with love, a roof over my head and *Apfelstrudel*.

CONTENTS

INTRODUCTION

WHEN THE HEART HITS THE FAN

TURN ON THE AIR CON

INTRODUCTION

When the heart hits the fan, turn on the air con.

I have escaped the Austrian Alps and ventured to London to fulfil my dreams, like every other Austrian comedian – which is just me, basically. What you need to know about me before reading this book is that I am in my mid-30s (probably late 50s by the time this book is published), I am a lesbian, I lied about my height on my passport (not by a lot, I just rounded up a bit), I hate watching ski jumping on TV, and I don't wear clothes that are made out of curtains. I think that's enough and we can officially start with the Introduction.

Maybe I should also mention that I have personally never read the introduction of a book, so I assume that other people skip it as well. In fact, I probably won't even read this Introduction, so excuse the typos you are bound to find,;?!.,. But, anyway, here are some of the reasons why I have written the best new Anti Self-Help book on the market (Romford Market) and how to navigate your way through this book-not-book.

First of all, I should say this book does help, even though it is an Anti Self-Help book. It really does. If you bought this book, I absolutely guarantee you, it helps. If not *you*, at least me. So, thank you, this book paid for my glass of wine tonight. If you haven't paid for this book, why not? Even if it was a gift, it should not be for free so please consider sending me a bottle of wine directly to make up for it. I will leave my email address at the bottom of this chapter, so you can send something over.

The concept of the book started years ago. I wrote about 30,000 words before my backpack was stolen. My backpack containing my brand-new laptop, my new phone, my keys, my wallet and my comedy notebook. A few thousand pounds' worth of goods and a bunch of good jokes: out of the window. It was a traumatic experience, being stranded in a coffee shop in the middle of London with nothing left, and only one phone number memorised: my own. I should have called the thief on my phone and asked him to at least share my friends' phone numbers, in the hope that someone might be able to rescue me or give me money for the Tube, a locksmith or a new laptop.[1] Which is what I did.

The owner of the coffee shop kindly let me use their landline phone. I dialled my own number, hoping

---

[1] I assumed the thief was a man. I feel a bit bad about that because I am normally against gendered assumption. But I did it anyway.

the thief would pick up. He didn't. The call went straight to my voicemail, which made me very upset because I didn't realise how stupid I sounded on my own mailbox. I had recorded it years before, but only then did I discover how poorly it had been done. I felt like I was listening to a caveman who entered the twenty-first century without any knowledge of how to use a phone properly. Besides my thick German accent and bad syntax, I could also hear car noises and ambulances driving by. Very low quality on all levels:

"Hello, this is Elise. Lea — WAAHH WEE OWW — for me a message and I will next call you back I — WMFFF (a sound like I was almost hit by a car) — available — BEEP."

Someone honked and the line cut off. No wonder nobody ever left a message for me. It sounded like I'd died. I also wanted to hang up, but I thought this was my only chance to get in contact with my thief, so I gritted through:

"Hello, this is Elise (I still can't pronounce my own name in English). *I am the woman you stole the backpack from* (I try to have better syntax). *If you have time and don't mind, could you please message me the contact numbers of Lauren, or Charlie? Or my Mother, that's fine too. Or Julia. Thank you. And wait, yes, you also have my*

computer. A brand-new MacBook Pro. You could get at least £2,400 for it. Don't sell it cheaper than that – it has two terabyte storage. Just maybe, before you sell it, could I ask you one favour? See, I haven't done a backup but I have an external hard drive at home. Maybe you could pop by my flat and transfer the data? The hard drive is on my desk in my room, which is the one to the left. I live in East London, E13 7LB, 8 High Street, Flat 13. You have the key, it's in the front pocket of the backpack... just let yourself in. I'd really appreciate that. Thank you. Bye."

While I was standing in that coffee shop, slowly losing hope that he would call me back, I suddenly digested my own monologue and realised that my book – *this* book – and its 30,000 words were also included in the missing backup. Gripping the landline phone and watching the sausage rolls on the counter being sold, I saw my life passing by. It was not only that I hadn't backed up my work. No, it was worse. I'd had a backup on my Dropbox which, just a few days before, I'd decided to delete. For no other reason than a *virtual* spring clean. I don't even know where that term came from. I had never in my life done a real spring clean. But I thought: "My computer is new and has two terabytes, I don't need to scatter anything on Dropbox, I will just delete everything from everywhere and feel clean and light after." It wasn't even spring. It was October.

My naivety, or should I say stupidity, squeezed tears out of my eyes. When I started to have a mental breakdown in front of the sausage rolls, the coffee shop owner was keen for me to leave. She let me log onto my Facebook to contact my partner to come and pick me up. I cried for days and still cry sometimes when I see sausage rolls. Even if they are vegan. They have become my Pavlov's dog bell.

With the loss of my backpack and my work came the loss of motivation. I couldn't imagine writing the whole book again, even the thought of writing anything ever again made me feel awful.

A week passed before I found out that Dropbox doesn't fully delete deleted files. I was able to recover my 30,000 words. Filled with happiness that at least my book was not lost, I was *still* unable to write. I couldn't finish it. I couldn't even continue it. It ended up in a drawer and had to wait for another year and another catastrophe before I was able to touch it again.

The second catastrophe came almost one year later to the day, in the form of a break-up. This could be a bit boring. Nobody died, there was no tiger involved, and I was still healthy. It was just a simple break-up, but still not the easiest – although, break-ups generally do not fall into the category 'the easiest'. I just talked to a friend of mine who has broken up with her boyfriend, and she said she felt free and happy for the first time in ages, and then burst into tears. They are controversial things, these break-ups.

My girlfriend broke up with me after a long-term relationship. I didn't see it coming because we were talking about marriage, children and her crush on my friend, who was also in love with her. Not sure how I missed the last point, but when the break-up finally happened – two months after she told me about the mutual love between my friend and her – I was surprisingly devastated. I lost my self-respect, my self-confidence and my favourite pair of socks. I am sure at least two out of the three are still at her place.

It felt as if I had never experienced such pain in my life before. Which is not true. A year before, the thief, who never called me back, pretty much pulled the rug out from under my feet. Earlier in my life, I was a sad, closeted lesbian – when I tried to come out to my best friend, she didn't want to best friends anymore. Of course, I've also had relatives pass away suddenly, which left me in the deep pain of grief. And when I was in hospital getting treatment for a slipped disc, a needle accidentally hit my inflamed nerve, which was a physical agony I thought I'd never recover from. I couldn't move for ages, was bedbound and had my friend shave my legs for me (priorities, I know). All these things were very painful at the time but, by now, I had forgotten the emotional or physical pain. They became a compartmentalised memory, some of them really funny comedy sets paying part of my rent. So, actually, I can't compare the acute break-up pain with these already monetised memories.

When my girlfriend left me, I tried not to be bitter. I did my best to stay positive and was trying to convince myself that it is possible to learn something from the relationship. I still think that. And, looking back, I can say that I've learned a lot from her. I learned English – a lot of new words, like 'cunt'. Well, yes, I am bitter. Do I wish her the best? Not quite yet. Maybe in a year or two, when I am fit and beautiful, radiant and successful, in a great new relationship, earning a lot of money, living in a big house, with a dog and a cleaner. Then, I will definitely wish her the best. I would even let her work as my cleaner, if she needed a job.

I was so hurt that I ended up having a break-up breakdown, unable to function unless I was snorting self-help books like cocaine. I listened to every positive affirmation that was out there, became spiritual, scientific and a party monster at the same time. I meditated at 4 a.m. in a nightclub, drank green tea with tequila and prayed to a universe-god while analysing the dysfunctional behaviour patterns of our co-dependent relationship. I tried out every piece of self-help advice that I could get my hands on: from finding my inner child to positive thinking, and from facing my fears to embracing freedom and peace. Some of it was even good advice; but, for me, I felt there was *always* something missing. I might have felt better for ten minutes after taking and trying the advice but, each time, I kept coming back to the realisation that life was still awful.

One of my big discoveries was that self-help books are a bit like Disney movies: after a really good story, you are left with an illusion of perfection. How do we live happily ever after? Nobody really tells us about the married prince and princess (or the princess and the princess, or the prince and the prince or the non-binary princeSs*). How do they actually deal with bathroom tension when the princess squeezes the toothpaste from the middle rather than the bottom of the tube and doesn't twist the lid on properly? Or her finding out that the prince is peeing in the shower – the shower she always has a bath in? And how do they sort out the shoe problem: when she keeps walking into the kitchen with her outdoor shoes on and he, being very Austrian, doesn't want shoes inside the house, only slippers, which are called "house-shoes" in German? And then they get into a fight because he is not really Austrian, he's an American claiming to have ancestors from Eastern Europe and therefore Austrian genes, which doesn't make any sense to her because Austria is not even part of Eastern Europe. Are they able to sort it out? Will one of them start having an affair? Will she file divorce papers? Or will the prince passive-aggressively carry on peeing in the shower while regretfully wishing he had never returned Cinderella's glass shoe in the first place?

Nobody tells us about these things. And nobody tells us after we've finished a self-help book what happens to our self-helped self. I have been there, at the amazing feeling of freedom, finally having found myself and regained the ability to see the beauty of the world. THE END! Feeling self-assured and content at the end of such a book is great – but what happens the day after it's finished? When I might dent my car while parking, even though I recited positive affirmations for me and the Mini for ten minutes before I started the engine? And when my new partner inevitably leaves me for someone else as well? What happens when I don't get the job I applied for? And how do I, as a free person, deal with a pandemic that locks me down on my own without being able to show everyone my newly gained self-confidence? How will people know I am confident when I am practising social distancing? Life doesn't stop at the end of the film or on the last page of the book. But it seems the advice for life does.

During my self-help reading journey, I noticed that a lot of people who write self-help books have personally gone through an awful time. They have been in the darkest place, walked through hell until they saw the light at the end of the tunnel and somehow found a method, a technique to cope with their pain, fear or tension and got themselves out again. That made me think maybe instead of *reading* self-help books I should *write* one myself. Maybe that is the cure, not to *read* other people's advice but to *give* other people advice.

I also learned that it's not essential to be a qualified psychologist or therapist. Anyone can write a self-help book: even the neighbour downstairs who can't manage to put his bin bag inside the wheelie bin, can come up with reams of unproven theories and advice. Not to forget the checklists of positive actions that make people feel guilty for not following them all, immediately. The gaslighting technique of self-help: creating guilt for not doing enough of it? Great for customer retention. The good thing with self-help books is that if the same book is published with a different title people will buy it again. Exactly the same people tend to buy exactly the same book within 18 months.[2] So watch out for my next book, which will be this book but retitled 'Frick'in Self-Help'.

There is no market regulation or qualification needed to write a self-help book. I even read a book by someone who teaches you how to cure homosexuality. I

---

[2] It's not totally made-up by me, Steve Salerno said this on *The Why Factor* podcast about self-help.

bought it, not because I wanted to be cured, but because I needed new material for my comedy show. This book was written by a gay man. An ex-gay man. He turned himself straight with his own methods that he now teaches to other unhappy gay people who don't accept themselves.

Whilst it didn't cure me, it was a useful moment of inspiration. I realised a fundamental thing about our self-help society: this man shared, like many other self-help pioneers, a story about himself, how he was heartbroken and depressed. His life was difficult and awful. Being enlightened by some god, he decided to heal his homosexuality as he became more and more convinced that this was a developmental disorder that led to his emotional unrest. He concluded that he needed to change his sexuality to make life good again. This man basically self-diagnosed, self-therapied and self-published.

After finishing his book, I thought, if *he* can write a self-help book, I can too. I'm pretty good at forcing my views on other people and I think my opinion is very satisfactory. I am also good at making universal statements without checking if they're actually valid. It's a self-help book, not a PhD thesis, so nobody really checks. And I also have a backstory: I have seen the darkest places for myself and walked through hell – maybe I can find a childhood trauma to add to the list too.

All of this, except for one notable difference: I haven't seen a light at the end of the tunnel. Not even a light switch. Nothing. I wrote this book in the dark, without any insight. I can't teach and preach and share great things about how to move on. And I am unable to heal all the broken-hearted people in the world; to mend them with my enlightenment, because I haven't had it yet.

So, <u>this</u> is the reason why I have called this the *Anti* Self-Help Book. If you are broken-hearted, sad or miserable, let's sit down together, have a cup of tea and share our miseries (you don't have to drink tea if you're not British. I will have water instead as well. I don't know why there is such a fuss about tea, but I had to mention it because I want to get a British publisher. If I didn't get a British publisher and haven't deleted this comment, I did forget to proofread).

I won't cure you with the methods everyone uses anyway, but let's have a laugh about awfulness and self-help methods, let's fail together whilst following generic self-help advice and not feel guilty that we skip the steps that might have, should have, could have made us feel better. And let's stay gay. In whatever way.

In case you don't feel miserable and are a happy person, you can either quickly do something that makes you feel miserable – pee in the shower or say something mean to your mother... whatever does it for you – or you can just read about my misery, and you will feel even better than you felt before.

If you have questions or positive feedback, or want to send me a bottle of wine, please email me at: wine@alicefrick.com. If you have any negative feedback or want your money back, please email me at: alice@spam.com.

1. ENJOY THE JOURNEY

Hopefully it's on a train and not on a donkey.

The journey is a path we take to get from one place to another: from being born to dying, from London to Thailand or from the bedroom to the bathroom. Everything turns into a journey, even if we don't have a goal. But, if we have a goal, a journey is still required to get us there.

To "enjoy the journey" is one of the most generic pieces of self-help advice ever. Apparently, happiness is a journey, not a destination. Really? Who came up with that? Have I missed something? Has every child in the world missed it too? As they are the ones who keep asking: "Are we there yet?" I know a Buddhist monk enjoys the journey more than the destination but, let's be honest, where does a Buddhist monk really go? Have you ever seen one on a crazy ride in an amusement park, skiing in the Austrian Alps or diving in the Galápagos Islands? Right. I think if you have more fun on the journey, you have chosen the wrong destination.

Of course, it would be lovely to enjoy the journey because that means we are able to stay in the moment, feel the present and live life to the fullest.[3] But we go on that journey because we want to arrive at our destination. We want to be at that pool in Benidorm, holding the lukewarm all-inclusive wine in our hand while fighting over the last sun lounger with a drunk German who claimed not one but seven beds before breakfast. We want to be *there* – in the middle of the happening. At the beach, the football stadium or the party. The journey is just something we put up with to get there. The journey is always: rushing, stressing, stumbling over, trying to get to or away from somewhere, being too late or too early or at the wrong address... When has the journey ever been enjoyable?

And that is only the physical journey. How about the emotional one? Having a death in the family, dealing with a break-up or fighting depression. Where is happiness in that journey? After a loss, do we ever wake up thinking: "Mmm, nice. How lovely! I am really happy that I feel miserable and sad. I'm enjoying the time it takes to get over my heartache so much!" The journey is hell. And if you are going through hell – I agree – keep walking. But, dear self-help books, please don't tell me to enjoy the journey.

---

[3] This is a quote from somewhere, I just can't remember where. It was possibly carved on a plank of wood in a gift shop in Devon.

While I was reading this advice in yet another book I'd spent money on for a quick fix, I spilled coffee all over my jeans, as if I had forgotten how to drink. Enjoy the journey?!

Thankfully, I was alone at home and nobody saw me sitting there in wet trousers, although Alexa might have witnessed the sound of my coffee slip. I was pretty convinced she had because, after my drunk discussion with her about British culture on a Sunday morning at 1 a.m. (I'm living the life), I've decided that Alexa is more than just a virtual assistant for playing music. That night, during our heart-to-heart discussion about me wanting to be more British, this virtual spy had ended up ordering an organic tea sampler gift box for £49 on my Amazon account, which I had to pay for! She may have asked if I wanted this gift box, and there is a possibility I said yes, but I was drunk! I don't remember! She was taking advantage and, not only that, ever since it happened the internet confronts me with tea advertisements. I don't even like tea! Since that drunken early Sunday morning, I have convinced myself Alexa's last name is Bourne.

So, yes, Alexa must have witnessed the sound of my coffee slip. As I so often do, I wished I'd unplugged her because suddenly I could see my Facebook being spammed with adverts for kitchen towels. Kitchen towels and organic tea? Honestly, what had I become? Where had the wedding rings and sex toys gone?

A journey is hard work. It requires controlling your thoughts; rewiring your brain; getting up, even if you don't want to; going to bed, even if you can't sleep; or writing a birthday card to someone, even if you don't really know them. It is *hard work*. Almost like going to the gym every day for months while nothing happens. Then, suddenly, after a lot of self-discipline and not giving up there are – finally – some muscles forming. Or a disc slips. Either way, something will happen!

An emotional journey is especially hard work because it's not linear. It is not like a train ride where you go from A to B. You go from C to F and then back to A via G. When you finally arrive at B you have already seen V and just want some tea (or coffee, if you're not British). Although to be honest, some physical journeys with National Rail feel similar. I once went from London Euston to Birmingham via Swansea after stopping in Glasgow. That was not due to the emotional breakdown of the train driver. No, it was just a normal weekend rail strike. These journeys are not straightforward and feel really painful (not only the National Rail ones). An emotional journey feels like a roller coaster ride on a donkey having eaten too much McDonald's.

However, I didn't want to write about something that I hadn't tried myself, so I decided that the next journey I approached would be filled with an attempt at enjoyment. I chose a physical journey to ease in. That was easier said than done, however, as my journey began with a sleepless night, because I had an early morning flight. When I have an early morning flight I either wake up every five minutes during the night, checking the time and my five alarm clocks, distributed all over the bedroom, or I don't wake up at all. Not even when the alarm clocks start ringing. One morning, I woke up and looked at my phone, which said: 9 a.m. My flat sounded like a birdcage with all the different wake-up sounds that must have been singing for hours. I jumped out of bed, threw clothes on and left the house before I realised there was no way I would catch my plane that was leaving at 9.30 a.m. And then I cried. Because that's what I do when things go wrong.

This time, I managed to get out of bed on time. Fully dressed, with a passport in my hand, I walked towards the Tube station. And it was not just *a* passport, it was actually *my* passport. I had a situation once as well where I was standing at passport control and the woman looked at me and said: "William Frick?" I had taken my Dad's passport and there was a split second where I thought: "Maybe, if I say 'yes', I'll pass and they'll let me on board." I didn't say yes. I just cried and missed the plane.

But that day, I had the right passport in my hand, and I ignored the fact that I stumbled over my own feet because my shoes were a bit too big, or my legs too tired, and I put a smile on my face when I got on the packed Tube to enjoy the journey. I was doing really well, but when I ended up with my face pressed into someone else's armpit, needing a wee and feeling the blisters on my feet, I decided to postpone my happiness until I arrived at the airport. Maybe the Tube ride was not the true start of my journey.

I started afresh while queueing at airport security. It was quite enjoyable watching other people struggling to take off their clothes. The Chinese man at the front of the queue was very serious about it and even took his socks off. But this was only fun for a while. After ten minutes I was not sure if I should get bored or angry as he was still standing there unpacking his laptops. His *laptops* (plural). They made me even more sad because I was reminded of my own laptop and suddenly relived the trauma of it being stolen. Feeling the symptoms of post-traumatic stress disorder creeping up on me, I almost had a mental breakdown in the airport security queue.

By the time it was my turn, I was emotionally exhausted but ready. Stripped down, shoes off, new laptop, iPad, phone, external hard drive and headphones in my hand – I felt like Shiva with his four arms and couldn't wait to get an airport security box to put it all in. At the last minute, I realised that I'd almost forgotten my plastic bag with all my liquids. I fished it out of my backpack, nearly dropped the new laptop, and was suddenly covered in moisturiser because I'd forgotten to close the lid of my face lotion.

People behind me got nervous because I took so long to get myself sorted after being so well prepared. Sweating – and moisturised – after giving my laptop a reassuring cuddle, I finally walked through the x-ray machine test, which I didn't pass. A strict-looking woman wearing gloves walked towards me. Without many words she touched my body. Suddenly, I felt scared and, for a second, I asked myself: "Did I bring a knife?" I have never in my life carried a knife. Why on earth was I now questioning myself and panicking that they'd find something illegal in my trousers? Her stern look just made me act more insecure and criminal. I felt guilty. I probably looked guilty. No knife found. Just a huge coffee stain on my trousers. They let me go through. My bag was still captured though. A young man, with not many words either, looked at me and asked: "Yours?" He had a tattoo on his wrist – I wasn't sure if it symbolised a bracelet or handcuffs. I was nervous again. Should I just say "no" and leave? What would they find in my bag? Did someone put illegal drugs in there while I was fighting with the moisturiser lid? Was the knife in my bag? Or was it him? Did this tattooed security guy plant something in my bag? All the criminals in films have tattoos. He looked suspicious. It felt like hours, watching this potential drug dealer going through my backpack, not finding a knife or bags of cocaine, but fishing out my dirty underwear until he finally found what he was looking for: the lip balm! The lip balm went through a swipe test, passed it and I got the box with the insides of my backpack back. Prideless and broken, I walked to the airport pub for a glass of wine and decided that my journey had only started then, after airport security.

As I was downing my first glass of wine, I felt more relaxed – although I was still confused as to why I packed dirty underwear. The wine slowly took the edge off my racing thoughts and my fear of flying. I am really scared of flying – at points so much so that I know if I was reborn a bird I wouldn't fly, I'd walk instead. But I had to fly a lot and the best method I found to deal with the fear was alcohol. After the first glass I felt better. Maybe this journey would be good after all. It was 6:40 in the morning and nobody judged me for ordering my second glass. Airports are good in that way. Nobody judges you if you drink at any time of the day. Nobody judges you if you fall asleep on the floor, holding an empty coffee cup looking like a homeless person. Nobody judges you if you wear five layers of clothes because you are only allowed an 8 kg carry-on bag.

I was finally having a great time and went for my usual airport walk to explore the free perfume testers at the duty-free shop, before I returned to the bar for my take-off drink, smelling like Eternity-Obsession-Number 5. Suddenly, there was complete silence. Not just in the pub – the whole airport was quiet. All the muttering stopped. I looked up from my wallet and saw everyone in the bar staring at the big TV screen. My eyes followed their gaze. That screen showed parts of a plane lying on the ground somewhere in the Alps in Spain. A plane had crashed. Just then. My heart stopped beating. I think a lot of other hearts around me stopped beating too. Even more silence. While they announced that there were no survivors, I heard through the speakers that my plane was about to board and that we should go to gate A12.

I didn't know what to do. How was I supposed to enjoy this journey when a plane had crashed right before my take-off!? I freaked out in silence. I was going to Austria to see my family. I like them, but I didn't want to die trying to see them. Ready to cancel the trip, I somehow ended up boarding the plane. I still don't know how it happened but, given the drinks I'd had, I reckon I just didn't find the exit and then forgot that I wanted to go home.

I remembered the plane crash again when I saw the pilot greeting the passengers boarding the plane. I am not sure why she was standing there, maybe to calm us all down after the morning news, or to look at us to see who she was about to crash into the Alps with. I felt the necessity to tell the pilot my concerns and said to her: "I am so scared of flying!" She just looked at me and said: "Me too." Then she laughed and said: "Joke! Just relax, have a glass of wine and all will be good." I said: "I've already had three!" At which she answered: "Me too" and laughed again. I'm not sure if humour is something to value in pilots.

The plane was really full, but I had a row to myself, possibly thanks to my Eternity-Obsession-Number 5 smell. Two Austrians were sitting behind me, and with every moment of turbulence they joked: "It's happening!" It made me laugh a bit, but I wasn't in the mood to be amused on account of the panicking. I took out my phone and asked the steward: "If I turn on my phone to call my Mum, will that increase the chances of crashing?" He said I was not allowed to use my phone and walked off. Very helpful. But I didn't really know what I would have said to my Mother if I had called her anyway. What was there to say? "Hi, how are you? We are crashing. Have a good day and give Dad a hug. Bye!" I couldn't imagine how that conversation would have gone, so I put my phone away.

While I was sitting on the plane, I realised that I was not sad about my break-up anymore – I didn't have time for that. I was too scared of being about to die in a plane crash. That was rather refreshing. The flight was a very long two hours, but I made friends with the Austrians behind me and the steward poured us a few wines. In the end, we managed to land on the runway and not in the Alps, which was a great relief to all the passengers. Everyone was applauding, even the pilot.

When I review my journey, I wouldn't say that I enjoyed it, but it did make me think – if life is the journey and happiness is only the destination we reach at the end of the trip, happiness basically means being dead. With that in mind, enjoying the journey is not just an option or advice, it's an obligation. A necessity. We must find joy in feeling awful because the final stop of our ride is the end of us. These two Austrians behind me were absolutely right: they needed to make jokes about the plane crashing because, if we crashed, we at least had one last laugh.

It might not be nice to stay in the moment, especially when thinking about break-ups or death or missing laptops, but it can be helpful to just feel the feelings of misery, fear and frustration. Why? Because:

"What you can heal you can feel." I need to look that up again... Oh, it was the opposite – "What you can feel you can heal." Which probably means – if you are scared, find some Austrians in the back row making jokes so you can laugh about your fear.

Not only that, I also found that staying in the moment made me actively forget about the break-up. For the first time in a long time, I was so intensely involved in the moment that I stopped dwelling on the past and the future that had passed. Fearing for my life felt amazing!

What is the conclusion of all this? Should we enjoy the journey even if we are facing another person's armpit on the Tube? Well, maybe we don't have to be happy every second of the journey. Once every two hours is enough (I think). Maybe it's not about enjoying the journey, but *embracing* the journey. Should we therefore embrace other people's armpits? Yes, because that will help us stay in the moment, which makes us become absorbent, strong and durable... wait... am I quoting a kitchen towel advert?

STAY POSITIVE

2. STAY POSITIVE

Good things will happen. Maybe not to you, but they will happen.

Being positive is an ability to stay in touch with your feelings, being self-aware and accepting the things that you cannot change. It also means you have passed a test, are pregnant or have Covid-19.

"Staying positive" is one of the most generic pieces of self-help advice ever. No matter what happens, just try to stay positive. Simple. But then, unfortunately, life gets in the way: phones get stolen, families are awful, people break up, countries get Brexited and coronaviruses break out. How should we stay positive then?

I think it is very easy to stay positive, when I am in a good place. With my friends on a beach in Bali drinking cocktails in front of a 5-star hotel? No problem. I can stay positive from the moment I hit the breakfast buffet until I hit my seven pillows in the king-size bed of the luxury hotel, falling asleep with the love of my life. But when I have experienced pain, rejection and isolation, I have checked into Hotel Sadness.

Hotel Sadness doesn't have good reviews on Trip Advisor, yet it's a very popular destination for the downhearted because it's so easy to check-in there. No reservation is required – they always have a free room. It's a place without windows and without perspective. No radio playing good music, just a stream of your own consciousness in a minor key. The walls are empty. There are no big, colourful pictures of happy people, stunning environments, *life* – anywhere. It's a maze without an exit. The only thing I manage to do in Hotel Sadness is to buy yet another self-help book. Somehow there is always a way to find a book shop with a self-help shelf. It's an addiction, a sugar rush, a rave party; chasing the high of 183 pages before I get hit by the comedown and feel low again.

In the latest self-help book, I read that human beings think 75,000 thoughts a day. *Seventy-five thousand?* That's just mad! There are 77,000 different viruses and bacteria on a public toilet – almost the same number as thoughts in my head! What do I do with all these thoughts? And what are they up to? Are my thoughts infectious agents who seek nothing more than to cause disorder, like all those toilet germs? What do we even think about in that number of thoughts per day? Are our ideas impressive? Revolutionary? Or just mundane?

Annoying? Too high-pitched? Ready to be flushed? Do I only think about pulling up my trousers again after going to the loo? Is that how I spend my 75,000 thoughts per day? The fact that I don't even know what I'm thinking is, perhaps, an indication that quantity is not a measure of the quality of my thoughts. Maybe all my thoughts are just wasted on things I don't need to think about. Although I wouldn't want to mess with my thought system and forget to pull up my trousers.

At first, I was really surprised by the vast number of thoughts that we all have. But then, when I was sitting in the windowless room of Hotel Sadness, I started to *feel* my thoughts. And I realised that I probably think not just 75,000 thoughts a day, but more like 320,000 thoughts in half a day. A constant tornado of memories, predictions, reflections and all kinds of emotions in the form of words whipped up in my mind. My brain had never thought so much before. Nothing could stop it from thinking. It was almost as if it had signed up for a marathon and realised it only had one week left to get fit and started running day and night to catch up on the training. It was the toughest brain workout ever. Brain gym 24/7. It got so fit, I was almost proud of myself. I could feel my IQ rising. I think my head size even got bigger. If you saw me in the street, my head would have looked huge and my body really tiny!

The only problem was most of these thoughts were negative and repetitive – no world cure, Nobel Prize material or TED Talk nomination. Just negative thoughts that would not find solutions to budget cuts or novel viruses. Nor would they invent flying shoes or explain the design of the universe. Nothing. They weren't even mundane enough to remind me to pull up my trousers after going to the loo. No, they were just voices that made me feel bad and talked down to me. My fit, muscular, overworked brain couldn't use its strength to get me out of Hotel Sadness. Instead, it used its new-gained muscle power to lock the exit door – again.

Once I realised this – which, luckily, happened quite quickly within my 320,000 thoughts in half a day – I decided that it would be best to put a stop to these thoughts. To shut them up. So I rolled up a ten-pound note and snorted another self-help book for more advice: "Keep moving", it told me.

It was worth every penny because, as soon as I started to keep moving, I was able to shut my thoughts up. The more I moved the quieter my thoughts became. I went for walks, met up with friends, went to museums, yoga, wine tasting, ballroom dancing, clubbing, singing, swimming, spinning, swinging... and that was all in Day One! I needed to move a lot to shut up hundreds of thousands of thoughts. And it worked. I probably did more on that one day than I had done in the last 37 years of my life. The only question was: what would I do on Day Two? If I continued like that, by the end of the week I'd be dead. Quiet, but dead.

I kept looking for alternative solutions to keep my thoughts quiet without having a heart attack, and this is how I came across Louise Hay. Louise Hay was an author, a metaphysicist and motivational speaker who wrote books about how to heal yourself, your heart and your body while loving yourself with loving thoughts. Her work is all about affirmations, which basically replace negative thoughts with positive ones. Brilliant. That sounded way less exhausting than what I'd tried before. But it was hard at the beginning because the negative thoughts are really fast and strong. In the real world, they'd get pulled over by the police and issued one ticket after another. Maybe they'd even get arrested because they all seem to be on speed and cocaine at the same time. The positive thoughts, on the other hand, are sloth-like! They move so slowly! It was unbelievable. They are like that person on the motorway who drives at five miles an hour in the overtaking lane while smoking weed.

I got the chance to practise my positive thoughts when I actually *was* pulled over by the police. I wasn't driving stoned in the overtaking lane, but I was accidentally speeding. Accidentally, because I had no idea what the speed limit was. At first, I didn't notice that the police were following me. The music in my car was so loud that I didn't hear the sirens. After a while I registered the police car in my rear-view mirror. I felt excited and wanted to watch who they were chasing. I looked around, saw no other cars and realised... it was me. Louise Hay's affirmations came to mind: "I love myself. I accept myself. I approve of myself". I pulled over. The police officer looked at my driving licence and asked me: "Do you know the speed limit here?" I said: "No." Perhaps I was being too honest and negative. She pointed at a sign that was literally in front of my car and read: "Thirty miles per hour." I cringed. The officer asked me if I knew how fast I was driving. I guessed: "Seventy?" She shook her head: "You were driving at forty miles per hour." I smiled optimistically and said: "That's not too bad!" She didn't like me being positive and wrote something on a piece of paper while mumbling that it would cost me £100. That is a lot of money, especially for a comedian. I asked for a discount, but she ignored my request. Nevertheless, I stayed positive and told her that I would pay the money, but I did ask: "Would you mind taking a selfie with me? I might be able to sell the photo on my website." She refused. I tried again, and we finally agreed that I could take a selfie with the police car instead. The officer handed me the ticket and I handed her the flyer for my next show along with my social media handles.

I was proud of myself that I'd managed to stay positive. I still had to pay the fine, but I might have gained a new follower on Instagram. And I was sure there was a glimpse of a smile behind her serious expression.

Being positive doesn't prevent you from getting a speeding ticket or losing money but positive people are happier, funnier and give more in tips. I don't think it's possible to check-out of Hotel Sadness after just one positive experience, but the good thing was that I could go back to my windowless room and hang up my selfie with the police car and my £100 fine. Suddenly my room looked much brighter. If you are not positive yourself, try to collect positive memories to decorate the misery. It's a small step but, after a few weeks of redecoration, every room in Hotel Sadness can be transformed into a quirky boutique hotel and win the Channel 4 show *Four in a Bed*.

If you can't love yourself, at least listen to Louise Hay loving herself. It is really nice to hear how happy some people are with themselves. And this is the key, I think: if you don't feel positive, be sure to surround yourself with positive people, because positive people give you energy, inspiration and reduce the risk of death from cardiovascular disease.

FIND

A

NEW HOBBY

3. FIND A NEW HOBBY

Have fun. NOW!

A hobby is something fun you do on a regular basis in your leisure time – not to be confused with something that is too much fun, like getting drunk or watching Netflix. It's more active, like playing an instrument – which, most of the time, is not fun, like when you have to learn scales or sight-reading. Basically, a hobby is something you love which is hard work, tiring and expensive. But it is good to have a hobby because, as Rihanna said: "I may be bad, but I'm perfectly good at it."

Every time an emotional asteroid hits my life, it feels like everything stops. Well, not everything, utility bills keep on coming. But everything else stops. Sometimes even Louise Hay's voice stops. The future becomes a distant memory, and the past is buried under a thick blanket of sorrow – like Pompeii being covered in millions of tons of volcanic ash. Or a sticky toffee pudding that is covered in custard. Or human hands covered in hand sanitiser.

It's as if someone pressed the pause button during the second act of a movie. After I have crossed the threshold and accepted my call for adventure with all my friends and enemies, suddenly, it all stops. The story can't conclude. The writer has put down her pen without finishing the third act. There is no end anymore, no revelation after the final battle. There will not even *be* a final battle. I have to start a new story without knowing any of the other characters or my own goal. I need to find a different antagonist whilst I am not even sure if I am still the protagonist in this new film.

The one positive thing, when everything stops all of a sudden, is that I realised bad things also stop. After my break-up, my hypochondria stopped. Just like that. On pause. I suddenly didn't think I was dying of a cold anymore, which I always assumed was a tumour behind my nose with metastases inside my throat. I didn't have to wake up in a panic, like I normally do once a month, thinking that my period pain was a ruptured appendix which would cause me to die of septic shock. I stopped reading the patient information leaflets for pills I didn't take and stopped developing side effects I couldn't get. It just all stopped. It was on pause, like the rest of my life.

But then, of course, when everything is paused you have so much more time on your hands. With the pressure of having to enjoy the journey and staying positive, it feels like you need to occupy yourself, to not let any negativity take advantage of that moment of stillness.

My self-help collection recommended finding a new hobby. I won't say it again, but this is more generic self-help advice, which literally means: don't be miserable alone, go out and be miserable with other people while doing something you think you like. The problem was that I had to find "something I think I like" at a moment in my life when I hated everything. Why would I want to go out and meet new people when I could just stay at home alone and be inconsolable? The only human contact I could bear was the delivery man from Uber Eats who brought me another bottle of wine with my lukewarm, floppy vegetarian duck dumplings. What was my hobby? Had I ever had one? I seemed to have forgotten about it, and the idea of finding a new one had already exhausted me. The misery made me indecisive. I didn't know what I wanted. I didn't want to remember what I had wanted. And I didn't know why I didn't want what I should have wanted. This hobby pressure was pure distress. Besides the normal crises, I had opened up a whole new can of worms with the label 'existential crisis'.

Telling me to find a new hobby was almost as useful as telling a depressed person to be optimistic. This only makes them feel worse as they realise that everyone else can see the beauty of the world except them, therefore, something must be fundamentally wrong with them for not being able to see it too.

However, I stopped arguing with myself as to why I didn't want to find a new hobby – although I probably would have won the argument – and made myself do something because everybody recommended it. Yes, I would also have jumped out of the window had it been a suggestion in a self-help book, guaranteed to make me feel better.

Since I didn't know what my hobby was, I asked my friend: Google. Google showed me seventeen different hobbies to choose from. Number one: try out a new exercise class, like pole dancing. Great. The excitement was contained.

On a cold day in January, I attended my first pole dancing class. Half-naked and still sad, I swung my stiff body around a hard, cold pole, getting bruised and watching myself in the mirror, baffled at how I managed to transform every sexy exercise our teacher showed us into an awkward movement that was not quite *clownesque*, yet neither funny nor sexy. It looked like I didn't just have two left feet, but three, realising that one of them was actually my hand. I could not escape my reflection – there was a mirror on every wall in that room. And I dared not look up as I was convinced I'd find another mirror hanging from the ceiling. I decided pole dancing was better for people who were happy with themselves and not crawling around with no self-worth. So, I swapped the class for a glass of Baileys and Netflix.

Peeling myself off the couch again the following week, I decided I had always liked improv, and made myself go to an improvisation class. The room was filled with happy energy, and even happier people, and I already knew I wanted to go home. But I stayed. I played a racoon who was buying a bag of crisps from a vending machine. Nobody laughed. It was painful. I really didn't want to be a racoon that day. Then I had to play a woman with the physicality of a cat. I was also not in the mood to be a cat either. Finally, I had to enter the room and say "Hello" with as many different characters and emotions as possible for one minute. Each of my characters was sad, I was thinking of sticky toffee pudding and wished I was at the pole dancing class instead. I had always loved improv, but I realised that I couldn't love it in that moment. I dragged myself home onto my couch, desperate to be left alone to wallow in my own misery. But something inside me didn't let me rest on that couch. I kept hearing a voice in my head – a mixture of Louise Hay, Eckhart Tolle and

Rihanna. This voice made me get up and find yet another hobby.

The following week – football. There was a football group which was known for having friendly members. I had never been before, and new groups tend to make me awkward socially. I have done stand-up comedy for more than ten years, but I can't manage to interact normally when I meet a group of new people for the first time. One person or two people is fine, but a group is just too much. They scare me, no matter how nice they are. I get insecure, overthink what they think of me, try to make up for that and work on my relaxed look, which always makes me forget to listen to the actual conversation. It is very difficult. However, I gritted my teeth and got dressed to leave the house for my new hobby. They played outside in the park. The fresh air was good, but it was still January. I was freezing in -5°C, running around after a ball. I realised that I'm quite good with a ball – I passed very precisely. Always to the wrong team, but very precisely. There were a lot of new people, new names. I remembered Jen and Sophie and, for about half an hour, I thought that "Stay on Millie" was an actual name and not an instruction.

My social awkwardness was kept to a minimum as everyone was focused on the game. I was preoccupied with keeping moving, so that I didn't freeze to death as well as with running away from heading the ball after the first one got me. I hate heading balls. Headers? They scare me. They are horrific. Who invented them? It's forcing a concussion on yourself to run towards a ball that hits your skull at too many miles per hour and shakes your brain so hard that you see little stars. If my hypochondria had not been on pause, I would definitely have suspected a subdural haematoma or a cerebral venous sinus thrombosis. Every time a ball was high up and wanted me to head it, I ran as fast as I could in the other direction.

It turned out that football was able to help me forget my misery for ninety minutes. That was a pretty revolutionary discovery. Finally! Something that gave me a bit of a break, plus a bit of joy. Not like my flight, which also gave me a break but replaced sadness with fear. The misery, of course, came back after football, as soon as I got home, but at least there were ninety minutes of almost-fun in my life.

My first conclusion on hobbies: I don't like them. Nor travelling, or any other activities. Nothing really. When you don't feel like it and you do things that you *should* like, you literally make them worse. And I became convinced that you start hating the things that you *could* have liked too. Therefore, I don't think it's a good idea to force a hobby on someone who is not ready to be happy. It's like asking our depressed friend to be optimistic.

On reflection, getting off the couch and out of the house, even if I didn't enjoy myself, gave me at least another perspective. And other problems, like social awkwardness and heading balls. I think the big mistake of self-help books is that they lead you to believe the hobby will be fun. Nothing is fun when you don't feel happy, especially when it is a freezing cold day in January. But it does create a memory. A new neutron pathway. Or neural pathway. I have no idea what the right expression is – I am not a biologist or neuroscientist and I'm too lazy to do research, so don't quote me on that. Something forms in your brain: a new pathway of something that starts with an 'n'.

After I'd created a memory – new connections with people like Stay on Millie – I also went on holiday. It didn't make me happy at the time either; but, looking at the 3,000 photos, I remember the beauty of that journey – the spectacular waterfalls and the incredible landscape. With every recollection of that memory, I seem to forget the emotional pain I was in at the time. The pain became a faded reminiscence, not able to be revisited with the same cruelty as when it happened. I think that while we wait for a pain to fade, we should ignore the promise of how a new hobby will change our lives. We should just take that pressure away and start it regardless. And start and stop as many hobbies as we need to go through this process. In the best case it doesn't matter because nobody dies doing hobby-ing. Unless you go hunting and end up shot. So better not do that. No hunting.

Maybe the film is not on pause and life is not a perpetually unfinished script. Maybe it's just really bad writing that lacks a good storyline, or a pile of incomplete scenes. When we think we're in another movie and have to start anew, it is, in reality, the same film and we are still the protagonist. What felt like a pause was just another scene with a genre change. A French avant-garde film that didn't make any sense at first, and even less sense as it goes on, ending with Rihanna, played by Catherine Deneuve, suddenly appearing in the dark whispering: "I may be bad, but I'm perfectly good at it."

As a warning though: the downside that came when I found more fun in my hobbies was that I also began to read patients information leaflets again. I did suffer imaginary thumb cancer the other week, triggered by an overexposure to iPhone radiation because I was texting a lot with Stay on Millie about a football tournament. My hypochondria has been restored to its former glory.

SAY
NO

4. SAY NO

Yes. Already wrong.

The word "no" is important to establish boundaries. It gives clarity. It can take away opportunities but also brings self-confidence if these opportunities turn out to be bad choices. Saying no can feel like a rejection and a refusal, because it is one. It can make you feel guilty, because sometimes you should feel guilty. But at least it keeps your workload balanced.

    I often know what I want (unless I'm obliged to find a new hobby) and, in general, can make decisions quite quickly. I go to the supermarket, look at the bananas and know which banana I want. But it stops right there. Literally, right there. I know my bananas, but suddenly feel pain in my heart – the pain of having offended the banana next to my banana: the Fairtrade banana that is already a bit squashed with brown spots. I don't want her, but she gives me these sad banana-eyes and it breaks my heart. How can I not want her? Shall I just take her instead and reject my banana? How does my banana feel about that? To be exchanged the moment after she had been chosen. 'It's a heartache'. 'I am lost'. 'Caught in the middle'. 'Straight from the heart'. Ready to write a sad song about it.

This was me on a Thursday at 10 a.m., standing in front of the banana shelf, in an empty supermarket, feeling torn while staring at upset Fairtrade banana-eyes. Of course, I bought her. I bought both of them and got the hell out of there before any other bananas could give me a look and throw me into a co-dependent relationship, which I never thought was possible with a piece of fruit.

And, of course, it doesn't stop with bananas. I remember as a child it took me hours to go to bed. Not because I wanted to stay up. No, because I needed to kiss all my toys goodnight. And I am a post post-war child: I had a lot of toys. It was nearly midnight before I could finally close my eyes, fall asleep, and get a few hours rest before I had to go to kindergarten and kiss every toy good morning again. It was a stressful life.

Cuddly toys, bananas, bosses, neighbours, friends, partners – the list is endless. You don't necessarily want to kiss them all goodnight, but it is the same principle: it is hard to say no to them when they give you sad banana-eyes.

Why do we agree to do things we don't want to do? And why do we keep having lunch with people we already know annoy us? Why do we stay in relationships that are not good for us? And why do we force ourselves to attend a family member's birthday party we don't want to go to? I've read twenty self-help books on this topic and they all came up with the same answer: because we want to be loved. We don't want to upset anyone so we can be appreciated.

Great. While I was biting into my mushy banana, I wished I had done more affirmation work to love myself instead of wanting to be loved by others. Louise Hay failed me on that one. But how can I change it? How do I become more assertive, stand up for myself and not give a Frick about what other people think about me? Is that even possible?

A Buddhist monk in a silent church would probably tell me: "Yes, it is possible! If you focus on yourself, find your inner Zen and don't go diving in the Galápagos Islands, then you'll be able to stay within yourself without getting irritated by what other people think of you."

But a Buddhist monk in a silent church probably wouldn't tell me that as they don't hang out in churches. And if it was a silent church, nobody would be speaking anyway. So, instead of finding my inner Zen, I've figured there's another way to make me stop caring what other people think of me. This way of enlightenment is called: alcohol. It is an ancient wisdom – the more you drink, the less you care. Of course, it might be argued: what about the next morning? Correct. It will be bad when you wake up. Dreadful. May be even embarrassing. But at least you had an evening off.

I've been there. Waking up feeling horrible *and* guilty, whilst having flashbacks of my drunken crazy self – remembering the sticky pint glass I stole from a pub by hiding it underneath my tight tank-top. There was no way the pub landlady would not have noticed me pretending to be pregnant with one of her glasses. Sadly, I also recall another night, when I discussed school uniforms after a second bottle of wine, in which I mistakenly thought that comparing the benefits of wearing a school uniform with the Nazi regime would help me to win the argument. Somehow, I also recollect a drunken night in my early twenties when I jumped into a pool in a friend's garden, with all my clothes on (thank god, actually!) and ended up vomiting in my parents' car when they picked me up. Yeah, I have been there, and it was bad to wake up afterwards. But then again: at least I had an evening off. And waking up the next morning, worrying about what people thought of me, felt almost justified and right! After such a crazy night, I should understandably have worried about how I am perceived!

Besides drinking alcohol and consulting monks, I did discover another 'trick' to help me stop worrying about what other people think of me. The trick is basically to make other people look worse. Instead of making yourself feel small, make other people feel small. I tried this as well.

The first step is a simple exercise you've probably heard of – if you have a presentation and are worried about what the audience may think of you, just imagine them naked. What a great piece of advice! Who came up with that idea? Call me prudish, but I really don't want to see my audience members naked. I am glad everyone wears clothes. I don't even want to see them in their bathing suits. I don't want to see men in Speedos, holes in socks, or body hair on beer bellies. Clothes are great. They are there for a reason. Let's keep them on, shall we? Even in our imagination.

Ever since I heard about this exercise, I've become more stressed. Not only because I don't want to see most people in just their pants (or less) but, now, when I'm sitting in an audience, innocently watching a show, I suddenly wonder if the performer is imagining me half naked! I can't help thinking: "Have I shaved my legs? Am

I wearing matching underwear? Did I cut my toenails?" While I'm panicking, in parallel, I feel upset because I'm a feminist. Why should I worry about my hairy legs for a performer who is not even that funny? And since when do I actually care about matching underwear? This advice for sure doesn't help me, it just makes me feel worse.

But I've finally found a way that agrees with me more. My anti self-help advice on how to say "no" and stop fretting over what other people may be thinking about you is – start *overthinking*. Go into brain overdrive. Freak yourself out and create the worst possible scenario. It's like the man in the elevator. I'm not sure if you know this story but, for Austrians, it's what we grow up with. It goes like this:

A man, who lived on the 12th floor, woke up and realised that he didn't have any bread (this is a big deal in Austria. You *need* bread. And cheese). It was a Sunday, so all the shops were shut (they still are on every Austrian Sunday. Utterly useless!). It was also a public holiday weekend, so his neighbours were away. There was only one resident in the whole building, who lived on the ground floor. Our man from the 12th floor decided to go down to the resident on the ground floor, knock on the door and kindly ask for two pieces of bread. While he was waiting for the elevator, he thought about the question he was going to ask the resident. Perhaps something like:

"Hello, I am really sorry, but could I have two pieces of bread please?". He got into the lift and while it was going down he rethought the question: "Maybe I should drop the 'I am really sorry' part, because I sound like a beggar. I will just say: 'Hello, could I have two pieces of bread please?'" Our man was passing the 9th floor and rethought the question again: "No, maybe, 'Hello' is too formal and makes me sound weird. I will just say: 'Two pieces of bread, please.'" Passing the 7th floor, he thought that two pieces might be too much and reframed the question: "One piece of bread, please." He eventually dropped the 'please' because it made him sound childish, he figured. When he finally arrived on the ground floor, he knocked on the resident's door who opened it with a friendly: "Hello." And our man shouted at him: "You know what? I don't need your fucking bread!", turned around and walked off.

The neighbour was indeed a bit surprised. But, hey, our man said "no" to bread. That's a start! And if you overthink every situation you're in, you will end up saying "no" as well. You will become independent, assertive and a bit of a dick, which is – from what I've observed – a great indicator of no-saying people.

Don't worry, I have a plan B too. If you don't want to try overthinking, there is one more method I can offer – saying "yes" instead of "no". I know how this sounds. It sounds like I haven't solved the problem. But I have. The only thing you have to do is say "yes" to the person you want to say "no" to and then find someone else who struggles to say "no" more than you do. For instance, let's say someone at work forces extra tasks on you, and you can't say "no" so you end up with a huge assignment that doesn't fit into your already packed schedule. Just find someone as weak, or weaker, than you and ask that person – who you know can't say "no" – to complete the extra tasks for you. Pass the work on. Just like that. It's fantastic because the people who you think would hate you if you said "no", won't hate you because you said "yes". And the people who have even less self-worth than you, and took the extra tasks off you, won't hate you either because they tend to hate themselves instead.

The next time I go to the supermarket I will choose the busiest time and look out for a hesitant person. I will sneak up behind them and just say to myself, loud enough: "Aw, nobody wants to buy these poor squashed bananas. These sad banana-eyes break my heart!". I am one hundred percent sure this person will buy the bananas and I can finally walk home, guilt-free with a green, underripe banana. Just the two of us.

SAY
YES

5. SAY YES

No! Wrong again.

Saying "yes" is an important way to get out of your comfort zone and broaden your horizons. But it opens up opportunities that might turn out to be bad choices and lead to a loss of self-confidence. The word yes is good when you want to get married and bad when you set up a direct debit with a street fundraiser for the sister of a koala bear in Seattle.

Saying "no" is not the only tip you find in self-help books. A few chapters further on in such a book you often find another piece of advice: "Saying yes". It is a bit annoying after spending so much time learning to say "no", to discover that saying "yes" is the way to go.

Besides the fact that I ingeniously merged both pieces of advice into a single recommendation in the previous chapter, I wanted to explore the possibility of saying "yes" and really meaning it. For inspiration, I rewatched the film *Yes Man*, which was rather threatening because I felt like I became Jim Carrey and took Terence Stamp's lines very personally:

> *"You say 'no' to life and, therefore, you're not living. You make up excuses to the people around you and to yourself. You're stuck in the same dead-end job you've had for years... you lost the love of your life because she couldn't be with someone who didn't live theirs."* [4]

Suddenly scared that I was missing out on life, I wanted to shift my focus and urged myself to accept the challenge of the "yes" approach. There were probably many people and opportunities I'd already missed, because I didn't embrace the world with my head nodding. Motivated and full of FOMO[5], the following week I started with as many yeses as possible. I said "yes" to extra sugar in my coffee. I said "yes" to a flyer from an evangelist in front of my local Tube station who shouted: "Jesus will save you". I said "yes" to doing a free comedy gig in the deeply right-wing countryside where people fell silent at my lesbian jokes, instead of laughing at them. I said "yes" to the Black Friday deal on Amazon and "yes" to sleeping in on a Monday morning.

---

[4] https://www.quotes.net/mquote/132899

[5] FOMO = Fear of Missing Out – I learned this abbreviation on IG, which is apparently short for Instagram (so much to learn!).

I said "yes" to picking up the phone when my Grandma called and "yes" to her suggestion that I should've become a tax advisor. And I agreed that "yes" I should have married her neighbour's grandson fifteen years ago, who was now pregnant with his third child with the other neighbour's granddaughter. Well, his wife was pregnant, not him. Unless he was a trans man, which suddenly made him way more interesting and attractive to me.

This was also the week when I said "yes" to being part of a production meeting about a script that I hadn't read. The producer for this project had asked me to be involved ages ago and for a long time reading the script was at the top of my list. Yes, I had a list – but I didn't look at it. So, it was just sitting there, waiting to backfire on me. Out of the blue, the producer called me and wanted to know if I'd read the script, which I should have done by then. I could've been honest, but then it was my "yes" week, so of course I said: "Yes!". She told me the writer was in town and that they'd called a spontaneous meeting to kick-start the production and she asked: "We're due to meet at 2 p.m. today, are you free?". I bit my tongue and said: "yes" again, knowing there was no chance, no time and no ink to print out the script and read it. There wasn't even enough time to skim through it. I got dressed, jumped on the Tube and was suddenly aware that this could become a rather awkward situation.

When I arrived at the meeting, my first thought was that honesty would be the best policy. I wanted to tell them that I hadn't read the script. No excuses, just authenticity. Or perhaps a bit of an excuse... maybe I could throw in the printer ink problem? But they could have replied that I should have read it on my phone. While I was finding my words, everyone was on their second cup of coffee, and I realised that it was too late – I just had to go with it. I was trying not to look vacant, but engaged and thoughtful, but that was so exhausting that I forgot to listen to what had been said about the content of the script so far. I tried to break eye contact and started going through my bag to look for something – I didn't know what. A photo of a bearded man stared back at me out of the depth of my bag with yellow letters saying: "Jesus will save you". I stopped playing with my bag and looked into the eyes around the table again. Suddenly I got asked what I was thinking. I managed to repeat the last words that the camera woman had said and copied the facial expressions of the writer, hoping I would pass. I answered: "The ring in the garden... yes, I thought that was very intriguing". Nodded. Waited. Everybody stared at me. I nodded again and tried to look more serious. "Did you see a meaning behind that?" I was asked. I didn't know. Did I? "I did actually, yes. I can't quite put it into words, but something about love... or Jesus, something religious maybe?" Suddenly the writer took a breath and said: "Really? That's great! It could be an association with God, the fear of dying." He went on "I've received some negative comments about that bit because people felt it didn't fit the story; but, if you saw a deeper meaning, that shows me it works!" I kept my serious face and added: "Mmm". Then the conversation picked up again. It had worked! I'd passed! I excused myself and went to the loo where I collapsed in front of the mirror. I wasn't sure if I should be happy that I'd passed without being found out, or scared that the experience had brought me a day closer to my future heart attack.

On the last day of "yes" week, my friend invited me for a Brazilian. Why do friends do that? I didn't say yes directly – I thought I'd ease into it and work my way down, so I only agreed to an eyebrow threading. I will never forget it – and presumably neither will the woman who did the threading. As she looked at me, a thread hanging from her mouth, I wasn't sure if that was part of the procedure or if I'd interrupted her flossing. She didn't say a lot – maybe she'd worked for airport security – but just asked: "Eyebrows?" I nodded. She pushed my head backwards into the seat, stretched my closed eye lids and ripped my face off with that floss. Turned out, it was part of the deal. I screamed – of course I did! It was painful. I cried as well. I probably cried more than after my break-up, which was understandable because it felt like half of my face was missing. To my surprise, when I opened my eyes, I still had some eyebrows left. I looked around, expecting to find a pile of hair, but I couldn't see much of anything because my tears were still falling, clouding my vision. The woman, with the string still hanging out of her mouth, looked a bit irritated, but not too worried about my well-being. Then, very stern as before, she asked: "Upper lip?" Upper lip? Upper lip?! What did she want to do with my upper lip? What was wrong with it? I hadn't come for my upper lip and didn't think it had an issue! Or did it? Did my upper lip need a shave? What? Why am I now worried about my upper lip? I didn't even want my eyebrows threaded in the first place! Or did she just want to work her way down to my lower lip? She wanted to go for that Brazilian with her floss! I jumped out of the chair and screamed: "NO!" She stepped back and asked for three pounds. The pain in my eyes kicked in again. I gave her five pounds and didn't want the change, but a hug instead. She didn't give me a hug and pushed the next customer's head into the back of the chair.

Despite the pain and disappointments, not to mention sugar overload, during my "yes" week, I figured that I was quite lucky. My journey could have been worse. I could've said "yes" to an Uber driver I didn't understand properly and ended up working for a Mexican drug cartel. It's quite a big leap, but these things happen! Maybe only to chemistry teachers in *Breaking Bad*, but you never know! Although, on the plus side, maybe I would've finally learned Spanish and made friends with a lot of men with tattoos called José. And maybe my trip to Mexico would have been tax deductible, if I managed to show evidence that it was research for my book. But I could also have ended up in a jail cell in Guantanamo without my own Netflix series.

My conclusion after the week was that it is very good to say yes, but also very stressful. I'd totally recommend giving "yes" week a go, to figure out what you really want; but build in permission for a few noes as well because Jesus won't always be there to save you. Say yes to good things, like organ donation and equality, and to fun things like watching Austrian comedians. If you happen to end up arrested during your "yes" week and need to sue someone, don't sue me, sue Warner Bros. They made $223.2 million at the box office with *Yes Man*. I, on the other hand, probably earn five percent of every copy of this book sold, so you might not get too much from suing me. I can't afford a lawyer, but I hope this counts as a disclaimer.

find
your
inner child

6. FIND YOUR INNER CHILD

But be aware: It might be a grumpy teenager.

The inner child is linked to past experiences and the future. It is filled with our childhood wounds that we have not grown out of. It is egocentric and peevish and comes out when our loved ones forget to ring us back, or when we have to pay the electricity bill, or when we have to share our sweets, or when people keep telling us to be positive.

I talk a lot. I talk so much that normal people can't listen to me all day. I wake up and words gush out of my mouth like water from the Iguazú Falls. I think I even talk in my sleep. Some people would say that I snore, but I think it's actually talking. And when I am not talking out loud, I talk inside my head – there's a constant dialogue going on in my mind. Not just with myself, but with another person.

When I am in a relationship I talk with my partner. Constantly. Even if she's not there. Then I talk to her in my head, which is even more brilliant – talking to an imaginary version of your partner without speaking out loud. It's brilliant because they don't talk back! They just sit there, quietly, and love listening to your thought explosions. No opinions, no judgements, no corrections, just listening. It's great – I love it! It's almost better than talking in real-life. But after my break-up I lost not only my *real* partner, but this mirror image of her in my head. I really struggled with that. When I am not in a relationship, I literally don't know who to talk to, even inside my mind. Suddenly, I can't find a 'mind friend' who will listen to me. I feel that I can't waste their time, even though they're not real. I'm very British in that way – I become apologetic, over-polite, cut myself short and stop all think-talk.

After my break-up I became quiet and sad and thought: "Should I just not talk anymore? Shall I become lonesome, depressed *and* mute?". I was ready to feel unhappy and abandoned – even in my thoughts – but, after a few minutes, I couldn't do it anymore. I wanted to share what I saw and did each day – that I'd passed airport security while hiding a lip balm in my bag and didn't get caught; that I'd just bought another self-help book with a birthday card so the cashier didn't think it was for me again; that I'd been looking up dates when I could do my

English Proficiency Test, but had accidentally Googled 'English Proffeciancy' and was not sure if that disqualified me from taking it; and, that I'd given a homeless person a chicken sandwich, which he returned because he didn't like chicken. I'm a vegetarian myself, so why I got him a chicken sandwich in the first place, I really don't know. I needed to share all these daily incidents and irritations with someone – even if they were just inside my head. *Anyone* – even their avatar – to address them to.

In the self-help book I bought, along with an '80 and fabulous' birthday card, I read about the "Inner Child". I thought maybe *that* could be the solution. If I had nobody to talk to, maybe I should just find my inner child and talk with her. Who, if not my own inner child, would be excited to hear her grown up self's stories? It's a child, after all – they love anything, right?

The inner child can also be a joyful, playful little thing, waiting to play with you. That sounded great. I wanted to meet her. I was ready for her. I was looking for her. But I couldn't find her. Where the hell was my inner child? I started to read more self-help books, spiritual books. I listened to holistic YouTube talks, went for walks, and bought myself fun, silly things like a washcloth with a smiley face on it. Inner children apparently like these kinds of things. I tried to bribe my inner child; I begged, I cried, I cursed – but nothing!

It took me ages – and a lot of shopping at Tesco – to discover that my inner child was a little fucker, not cute or filled with joy at all. My inner child was an annoying, belligerent teenager, who had locked herself in her bedroom and wouldn't come out to play. I saw her, right in front of me, but she didn't even bother to look up. She totally ignored everything I said to her. How did I end up with a half-grown person going through puberty as my inner child? How did I miss the childhood of this ill-mannered adolescent? Where was my inner child? I wanted an inner *child* like I was promised in all those books.

Of course, she ignored my washcloth with the smiley face on it, because she didn't give a shit about things like that. She was interested in TikTok, Tinder, IG and... Louise-Hay-knows-what. But she definitely didn't want to listen to my story about the lip balm at airport security. I felt like a frustrated single parent with a monosyllabic teenager and wanted to quit already. What went wrong with the upbringing of that creature? And why did I even bother trying to find her in the first place?

But then, suddenly, as I was watching her ignoring me, it hit me: maybe she didn't respond because she didn't understand me. Yes, that could be it! My mother tongue is German but in my head I normally speak

English. Why? I don't know – probably in preparation for my English Proffeciancy Test. And yes, it's true, I only understand half of the things I say to myself. This led me to think: what if my inner child speaks German? I'd not seen her for as long as I could remember – especially not since moving to London – so maybe she simply hadn't caught up on the English lingo.

I started to speak to her in German – "und schau!"[6] – she understood German! My inner truculent teenager/child was not so grumpy anymore. She just hadn't understood me. It took her a while to fully warm to me, but she was actually quite fun when I got to know her. At first, she was a bit sad that I'd ignored her for such a long time. She was waiting in the lower chamber of my heart, but I didn't let her out. A bad habit – especially when I moved to London, jumped into a relationship and cut her off, completely side-lining her.

I hate it when people blame their parents for their neuroses, especially because – like me – they're often totally unaware of their inner children and the mischief they can cause. But my inner child was there. The whole time. She was there when I ate a gallon of vanilla ice cream in the summer and had blue, hypothermic lips for hours. She was there when I used the walls of my bedroom as a canvas, which the landlord hated. And she was there when

[6] This means "voila" in German.

I passed airport security with my undetected lip balm. We laughed. Then she got sad again that I'd forgotten about her. She said that she'd completely disappeared from my life and I hadn't even realised it. It was true. I hadn't, because I was living the *big* life – new country, new friends, new relationship. I didn't have time to play with her. I was just too busy. I felt guilty and apologised to her. I wanted to make up for it. The good thing about having an inner teenager and not a child? She drank alcohol. That helped. She liked drinking. I guess she was my kid after all. All in all, we had a lovely evening, talked about everything, had a good laugh. She also said she liked my washcloth with the smiley face. That was nice. I realised that she is quite smart really, possibly because I'd ignored her for so long. It had made her grow and reflect. She was very wise, had a quote for every situation of life and laughed about herself. I was proud of her.

I think that our inner children are made out to be much more demanding than they actually are. I've always found the idea of the inner child a bit heavy. You have to find it and nurture it, and most of the time it's wounded so you need to heal it. Given all that, you almost don't want to bother finding it. Way too much work! In reality, though, it was so much more relaxed, and really good to catch up with her. By now she has learned English so can listen to my daily thought explosions. Thinking about it, in a weird way, it made me grateful that I lost the imaginary version of my real-life partner because I *had to* look for my inner child/teenager.

So, if you're looking for your inner child, beware: she could be older now. Maybe yours is already '80 and fabulous'! If you have the same problem I did and your inner child is not responding, try another language. If you don't know any other languages, learn one. It might take a while to find the right language, but at least by then you'll have learned a new skill. That's not a bad outcome for searching for your inner kindred spirit.

The main thing I learned was – don't feel guilty about neglecting your inner child.[7] This often happens to inner children, but they get over it. Not only that, they get over it *and* learn from it. And they become so much wiser than their grown-up selves! Maybe they feel a bit hurt and abandoned, but they are pretty strong and durable. That sounds like a kitchen towel advert again...

[7] Disclaimer: Don't apply this to real children. You should not neglect them!

7. TRY THERAPY

A therapist is your single audience member who cannot leave.

Therapy is a treatment without the use of drugs. Sometimes drugs can be prescribed. It helps to conquer phobias, mental illnesses, obsessions and ex-partners. Therapy can improve the symptoms, but it doesn't have to. It is not a waste of money, unless it is.

Self-help books could almost be seen as an alternative to therapy. You could probably get eight self-help books for the price of one therapy session. Then again, self-help books are rather generic and either leave you feeling like you're floating through a Disney movie, only to crash land in reality at the end, or they make you feel worse with the pressure of dos and don'ts and having to feel happy when you don't want to.

I finally tried a real-life therapy session. Mostly, because my friends wanted me to. My inner child suggested it too. Having used them as an audience for months to dwell upon my break-up, they could finish my sentences for me and were desperate to walk out of my one-woman breakup show. I am still convinced it is a great story; but, even I agree, you can only hear it so many times before you get bored. I personally hate listening to other people's breakup stories. At first it is okay. But then, after weeks of hearing somebody chewing over the same problem again and again, I just want to put a gun in my mouth – or in theirs – to make it stop[8]. The whole world has moved on except that person. Wars have ended and started again (thanks America!), people have died and babies have been born; we have all got older. But it seems that the recovery for broken hearted people is an endless misery – a soap opera in its fiftieth year. Or the Ski Jumping World Cup. I'm Austrian. I love downhill skiing. But ski jumping – what on Earth is that? Where everyone looks the same and they ski down the same ramp – over and over again. No drama, no action, not even a tree. Just people in skin-tight salopettes with unfeasibly long skis, sliding down a ramp and taking off into oblivion. I'm even bored writing about it.

So, yes, it is really frustrating to see a friend not getting over an ex. There are 7.8 billion people in the world who they could date (minus one, as in the ex). And,

---

[8] As I'm a pacifist, it would only be a water gun filled with gin.

okay, thirty percent of them are underage, but as for the rest: go for it! You WILL find someone new.

Of course, these things are all too easy to say when it's somebody else. But when it was me whingeing, it was a completely different story. I didn't want to think about other people. I wanted to drown in my misery. I wanted to complain and moan. And, above all, I wanted them to listen. Being sad was one thing but being sad alone was awful. So I thought it was time to be sad with a therapist.

Seeing a therapist was a strange thing. I went to my first session, which was in my therapist's own home. I was sitting in the second bedroom that had been converted into a consulting room. The second bedroom! Who had been in here before? Had she lost custody of her children or did her mother-in-law pass away? Or was it an S&M studio? Was my therapist a bit kinky? She looked very strict and, with the right outfit, could have made a great dominatrix. The walls were quite thin – I heard every toilet flush from downstairs as well as a man clearing his throat. Was that the husband, a cleaner or a client who was a leftover from the S&M studio?

I really struggled to stop my imagination wandering off. And I also found the beginning very difficult. Nobody told me how to open a therapy session and it was especially tricky with a British person. Brits are much more polite than Austrians. Everyone always asks: "How are you?" – as in *everyone.* In the supermarket, on the street. They don't even know you, yet they ask: "How are you?", when they should ask: " *Who* are you?". There is only one answer to this question: "Fine, thank you." Anything else immediately causes confusion. This happened to me when I answered a lanky seventeen year-old Tesco cashier quite honestly: "Not so good. I just went through a break-up and my friends want me to do therapy, but I am not sure. I've never done it before. Have you had any experience of it? Is it worth trying?" He looked away: "Yeah, erm. Do you need a bag or not?". He didn't know what to say. Neither did the people in the queue behind me who were all suddenly consulting their phones. I realised that "How are you?" is not a question but a greeting. It's a phrase with only one correct answer. Don't freestyle. Don't be honest. You have to say: "Fine, thank you", and repeat the question to the person who asked you.

And always start your emails with "How are you?". Even if you are friends with the person you are writing to. I sent a Facebook message to my friend the other day, letting him know about an event and he called me immediately, asking if my Facebook got spammed because he received "a weird message" from me. Then he remembered, I'm Austrian and don't start any of my online conversations with: "How are you?". Make sure that using this phrase becomes second nature (this was a quick lesson for all my non-British readers).

But how do you deal with this situation in a therapy session? I knew the question was coming but figured that I couldn't say how I *really* was. But what would I say instead? Would the therapist ask: "How are you?", and if I replied with my standard: "Fine, thank you", would she then answer: "Brilliant, that will be £75, please"? Would that be it? Would that bring the session to an end? Would I be considered healed? Or should I say: "Good, thank you, how are you?". And then we'd talk about the weather. Or maybe she'd tell me how she was really feeling. She's a therapist after all, her business is all about feelings. Maybe she'd say: "I am not feeling well". And then I would have to spend my session on her problems instead of mine, until she cut herself off after fifty minutes and I'd still have to pay, even though I hadn't said a word. Or should I just say: "Fine, thank you... That was a lie. I actually feel awful. Can we talk about it?" This would be polite and stick the structure while moving swiftly on to the real topic without further interruption. Is that what British people do when they go to therapy? Or would I be diagnosed with multiple personality disorder?

I decided that it would be better if my therapist didn't ask me how I was. That's why, as soon as I sat down, I literally burst out: "I have some problems and need to talk!" It worked. She didn't ask me how I was after that. Maybe that's why Brits think that German-speaking people are unfriendly and too direct. It's our only chance to avoid the question: "How are you?", because we just don't know how to deal with it if we are not fine.

After I managed this first hurdle – and stopped being distracted by the toilet flush – I suddenly realised that the couch I was sitting on was from IKEA. I have spent too many years of my life travelling through IKEA, so I recognised this Nockeby three-seater sofa with chaise longue almost immediately. It has a memory foam layer, high armrests and a machine-washable cover, and it comes with a ten-year guarantee. What was that all about? Why did she want a couch cover that can be machine washed? What was going to happen in this room? On this couch? What kind of therapy was this? And what was with the memory foam? Why did she want a couch that could remember my bottom? I was also unsure whether it was a good or a bad sign that she shopped at IKEA. At least she knew how to put things together; but, with IKEA, there are always some screws loose.

I was attempting to get comfortable on the flat pack sofa, trying not to think too much about how many times the covers had been washed and why. And I tried not to think about it quickly because I remembered the session was only fifty minutes long, so you can't waste time thinking about things other than why you're there. £75 for fifty minutes – that's really expensive. For that money I wanted to get something out. I felt the urge to look good afterwards – I wanted an enlightenment, a revelation or a facial. But I didn't even have time for that because I did the maths before I saw her: if I paid £75 for fifty minutes, then every minute of talking would cost me £1.50. Everything I said to her *had* to be really well-thought through. If talking was going to cost me £1.50 per minute, it would need to be perfectly pitched and well-rehearsed. And it was. I came prepared. No "erms" or "ahs". No thinking breaks or staring into the mid-distance. I lost a few minutes thinking about the IKEA couch, but I got back on track and told her my story beautifully in exactly fifty minutes. Perfect timing. Not a minute over. I didn't give her an opportunity to interrupt me – I had a lot of punchlines and a great story arc. I used surprises, call-backs and left on a cliff-hanger. It was fantastic! Better than every Edinburgh Fringe show I'd ever done. I wished she hadn't taken notes but had written me a review instead. I was *really* good. She listened to me with her eyes wide open, in the front row. I made her laugh. I made her cry. And I provided Austrian chocolate.

It was such a good session, I was thinking of going back because Part Two of my story was even better. There were more interesting characters to introduce before a grand finale. I knew my therapist really enjoyed Part One because she asked me if we could book something in for the following week. But then it hit me: why was *I* paying for this? I should charge *her*. Or she could at least chip in.

The session didn't cure the pain of my break-up. But I was able to reflect on my story when I learned my lines for it. So, is therapy any good after all? Yes, you can say things out loud that you'd normally just say to your inner child. You make more sense of your break-up story than the lived reality. And like the unfinished script of life, when you decide which bits to tell and how to tell them, you become the ghost-writer of your autobiography. That is pretty powerful. It gives you new and potentially unexpected perspectives – definitely more interesting than a ski jumping ramp.

I guess therapy is a little bit like getting a cleaner – you get a cleaner and the cleaner comes to clean your dirty house. In the same way, people visit therapists and the therapist heals their sullied soul. But, then, there are those who get a cleaner and clean the house *before* the cleaner arrives, just like those who see therapists but do the work *before* the therapy session, seeking nothing but affirmation that they're on the right track. Some other people, meanwhile, get cleaners and clean the place *after* the cleaner has finished, just like some people go to therapists and need to do a lot more work afterwards. All in all, some of these approaches are more stressful and more expensive than others. Some are a total waste of money because if I clean my place before the cleaner arrives, why did I get a cleaner in the first place? At the end of the day, it doesn't matter how you clean it, how long it takes or how much it costs, because all the approaches have the same outcome: your house is clean – you just needed to decide that you *wanted* it to be clean.

If you do end up spending all your money on therapy, try to at least get something out of it. Ask for a discount, some food or steal the toilet paper.

8. DATE YOURSELF

You will pull. But you will also have to share your meal.

Dating yourself is a social engagement on your own, to assess whether you're a suitable prospective partner for yourself to have a romantic relationship with.

    I right-swiped myself on Tinder. Yes, I have two Tinder profiles. This happened because my therapist recommended I go on a date with myself. I'd heard of it before, but was resistant to the idea, so I decided to leave it up to fate. I set up two Tinder profiles and, if I happened to pop up on my own Tinder, I would give myself a chance. If not, so be it. Goodbye advice, no date with myself. But I did. I popped up. Probably because I was on the Austrian Tinder at that time, and the only lesbian on there.

    As I had never dated myself before, I was unsure what to do with 'me'. Where to take myself or what to talk about. I was also confused because I didn't know the difference between dating myself and taking my inner child out. There must be a difference because I can't date a child. For me that feels wrong – I am not Woody Allen!

To get ready for my date, I started with Google. Google had a long list of 'date yourself' ideas. There were also images, videos and news on the topic. But searching on Maps was fruitless: "Google Maps can't find 'date yourself'". It was booming everywhere else though – so many options! The trouble was, they all sounded depressing. And they *were* all depressing. Looking at photos of a woman next to an empty chair, toasting herself; or sitting on a beach next to a picnic basket, all by herself; or walking in the mountains, all alone. These women smiled in their aloneness. Depressing. Who took their photos? Who did they ask? The waiter in the restaurant? The kids on the beach? The mountain goat? "Excuse me, would you mind taking a photo of me? It's our first date".

While I was scrolling through these Google images and date suggestions, I almost wanted to yell at myself to get a life. Don't get me wrong, all the ideas were great – if I could've done them with another person! To keep motivated, I reminded myself why it's good to date oneself and consulted yet another self-help book... or two... or more. They showed me five good reasons to do it, and I'd like to share my personal treatise on the topic:

1) Dating yourself gets you out of your comfort zone

Let's stop here for a second. Do I really want that? And, if so, why would I want that? Why would I leave my comfort zone? 'Comfort' is defined as: "a state of physical ease and freedom from pain or constraint"[9]. Why on Earth would I want to leave that? For what? The experience of discomfort, difficulty, unhappiness, misery, sorrow, worry – get me the hell back into my comfort zone. Honestly.

Apparently, leaving your comfort zone enhances personal growth and eliminates fear. Well, in my comfort zone there was no fear in the first place! So don't make me step out of it to experience fear that I then have to eliminate. And personal growth? My personal doesn't want to 'growth'. It's 'growth' enough!

Actually, if I'm reading a self-help book, I am *already* out of my comfort zone. Something in my life has made me leave that space and put me in a state of discomfort, distress and fear. That is why I am reading a self-help

[9] 'Comfort', Encyclopedia.com, http://www.encyclopedia.com/literature-and-arts/language-linguistics-and-literary-terms/english-vocabulary-d/comfort, accessed 11 Oct. 2021.

book! I need advice on how to get back to my comfort zone, not recommendations on how to get out.

2. Dating yourself increases your self-esteem and worthiness

Really? When? When you go to a restaurant in spite of yourself? Order a table just for yourself? When you eat food all by yourself? Share a bottle of wine with yourself? Argue who's paying the bill amongst yourself? Stumble out of the restaurant all over yourself? When, exactly, would I have increased my self-esteem and worthiness? Have I missed something?

3. Dating yourself helps you to get to know yourself

I'm not sure about this either. I know myself pretty well: I am Alice, thirty-seven, Austrian. I know my bananas and I have lost my favourite pair of socks. I am hanging out with me 24/7. I know myself so well in fact that, sometimes, I get a bit bored of myself. I'd prefer to get to know other people for at least a couple of hours on a Friday night.

4. Dating yourself gives you time to reflect

I am on Chapter Eight of my Anti Self-Help Book. I've had a lot of time to reflect. I want action, not reflection. I want to listen to people other than Louise Hay. I want entertainment and fun. I want to have sex in the kitchen. Or maybe not in the kitchen – my kitchen is a dirty place with lots of unwashed dishes. It would take ages do to them before we had sex. And, even then, kitchen surfaces are really cold and hard. Maybe sex in the bedroom. Yes, sex in the bedroom would be good.

Reflection is definitely *not* at the top of my list. What would I reflect on when I go on a date with myself? How pathetic I am to not even have friends to go out with? Or how stupid I look, sitting there all alone?

5. Dating yourself is a great way to meet people

Ah! Okay. That basically means, if I date myself, I increase the chances of meeting somebody else? Well, that sounds good. That actually sounds very good. Why did I have to go through the other four reasons first?! A great way to meet people. Perfect. Sold. Off I pop.

After reading this last reason, I put on make-up and smart clothes and took myself out on a Friday night. I turned off my location service, just in case I was being monitored. I didn't want to be the first entry on Google Maps for 'date yourself'.

When I went out with myself, I realised there is a difference between dating yourself and playing with your inner child. Dating yourself is a lot more serious. It did not involve singing 'Head, Shoulders, Knees and Toes' and dancing like a dance-monkey. Instead, I was acutely aware

111

of my surroundings and tried very hard to act like an adult, which was definitely more stressful – especially on a Friday night in Soho, when all the restaurants were packed with people about to see a West End show. Everywhere filled up with audiences for *Harry Potter and the Cursed Child* and *The Lion King Musical.* There was not even a table for a single person available. I finally found somewhere – at the Angus Steakhouse. I have to admit, I was a bit disappointed with myself for taking me there because I was – and still am – a vegetarian. Yes, I appreciated that everywhere was heaving, but I could have tried a bit harder.

The entry was awkward, as expected. The waiter asked: "How many people?" I replied: "It's just us." He asked again: "How many?" I said: "Just us. Me, myself and I."

I got a table with two chairs and one menu. Then a waitress came. I ordered the only vegetarian meal on the menu: a salad, and a bottle of wine. She asked: "How many glasses?" I said: "Two!" because I panicked.

At first, I was trying hard to look as if someone else was supposed to come – checking my phone, looking at the door, pretending to wait. It got a bit embarrassing after I'd finished my salad. I realised that it felt even more depressing waiting for someone who wasn't going to come than to be on a date with myself. So, after the salad and the first bottle of wine I gave up. I stopped pretending. By then, anyone who'd been interested in watching me, because they were so bored with their own evening, must've known that the person I was pretending to be waiting for wasn't coming.

I treated myself to dessert and another bottle of the house white. At exactly 7:30 p.m., the restaurant almost emptied. Everyone rushed off to see Harry or the Lions. I was still there at 10 p.m., when the people who hadn't eaten before the show came in to have dinner afterwards. By then I was having a really great time. I'd found out that the waitress's dog was called Bobbie, had only three legs and was a rescue dog. I also learned that the cousin of the waiter was a comedian and knew someone who knew someone who was a really good comedy agent. And that this waiter's sister had a secret crush on the waitress with the dog called Bobbie. She was also a vegetarian, but used to come to the restaurant once a week to flirt with Bobbie's mum. I had a lot of laughs, three new Facebook friends and a Cognac. It was almost midnight when I finally decided to go home.

I ordered the bill and shared it with myself. Which worked really well as I had an English and an Austrian bank card. The waitress probably thought I was a bit mental, which was okay because I'd forgotten her name again. My English card tipped, my Austrian card didn't. A bit rude, but what can you do? Cultural differences. Outside the restaurant I decided to take myself home. A date with a happy ending. I'd pulled on the first evening. Nothing happened, because I'd had two bottles of wine and a Cognac. But we got McDonald's fries and fell asleep on the couch before we dragged us into the bedroom at four in the morning.

Was dating myself worth it? Just for feeling that I'd pulled at the end of the night: yes, it was worth it. It was also nice to wake up together the next morning. I had a bit of a hangover, and there was barbecue sauce on my face, but I thought that was cute.

At first, dating myself felt a bit scary, boring and expensive. But the more I drank the funnier I got. And while I was scared of people thinking I was crazy, I realised that other people are crazy too – like the waiter's vegetarian sister who visited the steak house once a week to flirt with her brother's colleague. I was not the only crazy out there!

I enjoyed dating myself more than I expected to. It was nice to make time for myself. And, I guess, when you go on a date with yourself, you already know what you're getting into. You have no difficulties remembering your name. You don't need to fake a phone call from your "sick" friend, if the date isn't going well. You don't have to pretend you like the food or the restaurant, or that you want to stay or leave. Because you will automatically know what you want and will have already agreed that with yourself. No fake smiles – and no drunken arguments about school uniforms and the Nazi regime.

What I enjoyed most, though, was the following morning, when I prepared myself a really nice breakfast, wiped the barbecue sauce off my face and made my bed. I never make my bed, but I wanted to impress myself – which was nice because I couldn't remember the last time I felt like doing that. Would I right-swipe myself again on Tinder? Yes, I actually would.

SELF-DEVELOPMENT

Pyramid of needs

9. FOCUS ON SELF-DEVELOPMENT

Learn skills you don't need.

Self-development is different from self-improvement – but they are both the same. Not only is there self-development, there's also self-help and personal development, but there is no personal help.

    In my opinion self-help and self-development are two very different things – but I might be wrong. I use the term 'self-help' for times when the rug gets pulled from under your feet or you fall into a hole – first aid for a broken heart. In these situations, it's good to do affirmations, find your inner child, ask Louise Hay how to enjoy the journey, say "yes" and "no", and be a racoon at an improv class every now and then. All this will eventually get you out of Hotel Sadness, but it will take time. In fact, time is much more likely to get you out than a racoon, but at least it's a bit more fun pretending to be an animal than simply feeling miserable. 'Self-development', on the other hand, starts after your wounded confidence has healed and offers activities and exercises that help you to grow mentally and get rid of bad habits.

Using self-development as the advanced level of self-help sounds very enticing – and logical. But I've discovered that, in life, nothing is truly logical. After school we can build on our knowledge at university. Logical, yes. But not true. By the time I'd finished my A-levels, I knew nothing about what I should have known, or it would have been useful to know. I knew that the waggle dance of a honeybee is in a figure-of-eight pattern, which the bee uses to share information about the direction and distance of flowers. I could also recite a recipe for tortillas in Spanish. But if I was the 'Phone a Friend' on *Who wants to be a Millionaire?* and had to answer a question on which countries border Austria, I'd fail. Badly! If I'd gone on to read Spanish at university, I could have recited my tortilla recipe, but I couldn't enquire about something or write a letter of complaint. I didn't even know how to ask for directions to the train station on a trip to Barcelona.

I don't want to blame my teachers – although I do – but I think that my Spanish teacher should have been less like Jamie Oliver and my biology teacher could have focused on a broader range of learning than the bee's waggle dance. She could have answered questions like: "How do lesbians have sex?" that would have saved me a lot of problems. Not necessarily for my own pleasure (although I'd have been interested to hear my middle-aged biology teacher's take on it as she was very old-fashioned) but mostly for other people. When I come out as gay during my comedy shows, this is the most frequently asked question. So, I do think there's a big knowledge gap and it would be great if that could be filled by teachers in schools and not over a drink in a pub after a stand-up gig.

I was only interested in studying *after* I'd finished high school and ended up going to university where I had to pretend to know things that I should have known already. This made me wonder if self-development was possible if I hadn't fully completed my self-help programme. I'm also wondering if there was a test I could have taken to see if I was self-helped enough to be able to move on. I didn't want to do another online psychology test that would've taken an hour and given me an answer that sounded like my daily horoscope. I wanted something quick and reliable, akin to the cotton swab from a Covid self-test kit. Would I be allowed to move on to the next level of 'facing my fears' and 'dating other people', if I didn't love myself properly in the first place? Was self-help based on Maslow's Hierarchy of Needs, where I had to fulfil one level before I could aim for the next? If I had a place to sleep and food to eat, could I then start to care about being healthy – mentally and physically? On the contrary, I found that once I'd satisfied my basic needs, I had more space and time to worry about other things – if I was happy, I could be a hypochondriac again.

The more closely I looked at Maslow's order, the more I disagreed with him. Obviously, while we have to breathe and eat before we can think about self-esteem, I also wonder, if self-confidence was at the base of the pyramid, alongside physiological needs, would this have made us better hunter-gatherers? With enough self-confidence, could we have lost our pigeon phobia and believed in our ability to catch one for dinner? Also along Maslow's bottom line is the need for sex before the respect of others. Don't get me wrong, I like sex, but not having it for a couple of days is okay too. Abstinence makes me cry a lot less than being belittled, yelled at or humiliated by others, so we could pop 'sex' a few levels up the pyramid in my view. The next point I object to is 'family' – I love my family dearly, but it doesn't need to take up so much of the middle tier. Once every two months is enough.

Maslow redefined his theory many times over the decades. Interestingly – according to some Google Books – he most recently revised it in 1987, which is a bit odd since he died in 1970. I'm not sure if he 'did a Jesus' and came back in '87 or if some authors, like me, are not quoting accurately.

In Frick's Hierarchy of Needs, the lowest level – the base of the pyramid – would be filled with: air, food, water and wine (who are we kidding... !), respect, self-esteem, freedom, creativity, health and money. The next level I'd fill with – sleep and sex. And, at the top, I would put: reproduction, family and clothes. I agree, this would not be a typical pyramid anymore – it would be more like an inverted cocktail glass.

I tested my theory by accident. When I moved to London, I lived an openly gay and free life with my girlfriend at the time in a standard London flat: a shithole. It was freezing, mouldy and, sometimes, creepy men peered through our bedroom window when we were about to have sex (they probably also had terrible biology teachers and needed to catch up on a few facts). But we didn't have bedbugs and it was in a great location. Who cares if your skin gets mould on it off the shower when you live only five minutes from the Tube? I loved that flat, my lifestyle and my girlfriend. Life was good. We were full of freedom and creativity. Until I got a call from my parents saying that they'd purchased plane tickets to London and wanted to visit me the following week. They knew how much rent I paid for my flat and, for that money, I could have lived in a five-bedroom palace in the centre of Vienna. So, of course, in my stories I always pimped up the flat a bit – a great two-bedroom place in central London, with a brilliant view of Tower Bridge, not a shithole in Zone 6. They also didn't know that I had a girlfriend – I hadn't come out to them at the time. In the Austrian Alps everything moves a bit slower than in London.

When they called me excitedly with all their arrival details, I panicked. My flat was not even a full one-bedroom flat, so there was no way I could make two bedrooms out of it. I would have to introduce my partner not as my flatmate but as my bed-mate. And if I cleaned off all the mould it would grow back within a few hours. The carpet had dissolved, the windows didn't shut properly and the heating worked for, maybe, an hour a day. There was no way that I could transform the flat to make it presentable for my parents.

Preparing for their visit was a full-time job. Suddenly, my amazingly happy life became a living nightmare. I was thinking of taking a mortgage and buying the place I pretended to have, or setting my shithole flat on fire so they couldn't see how bad it really was. I spoke with a builder to find out how much it would cost to make my flat more attractive, while fantasising about booking a flight to Las Vegas, telling my parents that I'd landed a big job and postponing their visit. Finally, I remembered that I was in my thirties and could act like a responsible, logical adult and booked an AirBnB. It overlooked Tower Bridge. Two nights cost as much as a month's rent, but it was worth it. When my parents arrived, I told them it was my flat and they were impressed. Not too impressed, as they expected something great, but still happy to see how nicely I lived. It was a bit awkward because I failed to get the shower to work. I didn't know how to turn it on and said I needed to call the landlord. Then my Dad discovered that you had to twist it instead of pulling it. I said: "Oh, really? That's a new thing..." As I was dying a slow death, my parents found men's clothing in one of the closets which I said were mine, just to take the first step towards coming out to them.

In the end, they did find out that it wasn't my flat. Until today, I'm not sure if it was because I kept being surprised by how the coffee machine and TV worked. Or that I didn't recognise the sound of the doorbell. Or was unable to lock the door in the evening: "I always sleep with the door open. It's a safe neighbourhood!". Or, maybe, it was the neighbour who didn't know me when we asked if we could borrow some sugar because I didn't know where I'd put mine.

In general, I do think it can work – faking confidence and achieving a lot just by pretending. "Fake it 'til you make it", as they say. I graduated from university even though, strictly speaking, I should not have passed my A-levels. Faking self-confidence is good – unless you are drunk and believe that you can still drive. Or fly like a bird. But most of the time, it is good. If you're confident that you'll win the lottery and buy a ticket, at least someone else will get the money thanks to your confidence.

When my parents found out that the AirBnB was not my flat, I told them the whole story: I came out to them, introduced my girlfriend and showed them my real flat. And the good thing was my shithole flat shocked them so much, they didn't even mind that I am gay.

The next chapters of this book focus on self-development. During the process of self-development – and devising Frick's Hierarchy of Needs – I've asked myself: What made me grow? What tools have I put into my toolbox? How can I spend my time wisely? How do I face my fear? Chase my dreams? And do I have to eat pigeon?

FACE YOUR FEARS

10. FACE YOUR FEARS

You might die. But you'd die as a hero.

Facing your fears means gradually exposing yourself to a distressing emotion – the feeling of danger or the risk of pain. It will evoke a psychical reaction, such as an increased heart rate, an overproduction of stress hormones and sweaty palms. By facing your fears, you'll feel less anxious about the fearful situation in future, but you might feel anxious about feeling anxious instead.

There is no self-development advice that doesn't suggest facing your fears. Fear is a very common emotion in human existence. It comes in many forms and shapes and has many different backgrounds. Just recently I found the literal 'shape' of fear in a newspaper headline — the fear of small holes called trypophobia:

"*People with a fear of small holes have claimed the design of Apple's iPhone 11 Pro is triggering their phobia.*"[10]

---

[10] https://www.bbc.co.uk/news/technology-49660765

There are people who are scared of iPhones? That made my day! Although I probably shouldn't laugh at other people's fears because I'm full of phobias myself, and most of them are irrational. To name a few: I'm scared of becoming ill, of getting stabbed (which is arguably rational given that I live in East London). I am also scared of spiders, Ryanair flights, toxic shock syndrome and Huawei phones (not because of the holes, but because of the spies). On top of that, I'm quite good at picking up fears. Just a few weeks ago, when I was on holiday in Perth, I visited the Fremantle Prison Museum – a World Heritage Site in Western Australia. Fascinated by the prison, I took the whole tour, which included a walk through the water tunnel system that was built by the prisoners. Before we began climbing down 200 metres into the tunnel system, we were asked: "Is anyone here claustrophobic?". I was not, and never had been, so I said: "No." Yet, as soon as we were climbing down the ladder, I caught myself thinking: "What if I *am* claustrophobic? How will it feel to be in such a confined space where you can't even stand up? No space, no air, no light, no contact with the outside world and – probably spiders everywhere! And the tour guide, she has a strange-looking face, she is probably a serial killer and can't wait to play Hannibal Lecter with us. That is, if we haven't died of heart attacks by the end of the tour."

Essentially, I wound myself up, thought I might die and had a panic attack, even though I was fully aware of what was happening. In parallel, I was scared of being scared because I didn't want to look scared – I didn't want to embarrass myself. Although I never cease to embarrass myself. For example, just recently, I showed up at my spin class wearing a bike helmet. I didn't do it for safety. I did it because I just thought that's what you did. I was sure that every time you got on a bicycle, you should wear a helmet. Full stop. That's what my parents taught me. How could I have known that there are different rules in London gyms? But then, I fell off the spin bike, so my bike helmet turned out to be quite useful in the end.

However, in that tunnel in Perth, I tried to hide my fear so as not to embarrass myself – again. I imploded my panic attack, while walking behind a happy American family and the woman who'd taken her chatty niece out for the day during the school holidays. I was terrified that someone would see that I was terrified, and even more terrified of being escorted through the emergency exit by our tour guide – whose name was actually Jane, not Hannibal.

Dealing with the fear of fear plus the fear of claustrophobia, I felt like I was in a multi-dimensional panic universe – let's call it a 'panic-verse'. It's fair to say that I didn't enjoy the tour. But as soon as we saw daylight again, all my panic dissipated. It completely dispersed as if there'd been no fear in the first place. Nonetheless, I didn't want to add claustrophobia to my list of fears because I thought the list was long enough already. So, I decided to look into it – to research fears and how you can get rid of them.

Google is very smart and hits the nail on the head. It says: "Fears restrict". Which is true, fears do stop me from enjoying my life to the fullest. Although, I am not sure how fully you can enjoy a tight, clammy tunnel with little air and no light. But I guess you could enjoy some features of the new iPhone 11 Pro if you were able to reduce your fear of small holes. My good friend Google also had a lot of inspiring quotes about fears. Like, a lot! The first one I found was by Bill Cosby, who said:

"Decide that you want it more than you are afraid of it."

Given that Cosby is a convicted sex offender, it doesn't give much credibility to this quote. Next? Marie Curie said:

"Nothing in life is to be feared. It is only to be understood."

A great quote... but didn't she do pioneering work with the invisible rays given off by uranium? And didn't she die of aplastic anaemia, which was caused by this long-term exposure to radiation? With that in mind, her quote didn't convince me to give up my fears either. Next? Marilyn Monroe:

"We should all start to live before we get too old. Fear is stupid. So are regrets."

Great! That'll do. With that, I shall face my fears. Or just one fear. Yes, maybe I'll just start with one. But let's go big. Let's go with... spiders.

I am, and have always been, terrified of spiders. I came out of my Mother's womb fearing the eight-legged insect[11] that crawls around floors and walls and hangs off ceilings. No one else in my family is scared of them. Just me. My Mother tried everything to get rid of my fear. For my third Birthday, she bought me a book about a little spider – one that you can touch with your fingers. It was lovely. I read it, touched it, but I was still scared of *real* spiders.

---

[11] ...which is, in reality, not an insect because insects, by definition, have only six legs; spiders have eight. What are spiders then? I don't know – I was too scared to Google it. (Editor: Arachnids).

As Little Alice I started a routine before I went to bed: I always looked up at the ceiling for the 'spider check'. Some people pray before they go to sleep, some people read books – I spider check, even today. It turned out to be a wise move when I was going to bed in a bungalow in Phuket. Looking up at the ceiling, a hand-sized, hairy spider stared back at me. You can probably imagine the state of panic I was in, given the fact that I'm even scared of little un-hairy spiders.

Despite being thirty-seven years old, it has never crossed my mind to face my fear of spiders. I just assumed there'd always be someone to help me out. Someone from my family was normally around, and that night in Phuket I called the hotel reception and changed the room. Easy. Even when I lived on my own in different countries, every time there was a spider in my flat, I found someone to help. Mostly by standing outside my flat, waiting for a neighbour, the postman or a random passerby and asking them: "Excuse me! There is a spider in my flat. Would you please come in and kill her?". When I was living in Paris it was more like: "Excuse-moi, une spidre c'est ici a la chambre. Entre, s'il vous plait". I am probably lucky to be alive, given all the strangers I've allowed into my flat.

All in all, until recently, it had never been a problem to find someone to help. Until 'that day' – a lovely summer's day in the garden. It was not even my garden. It was a friend's garden I found myself alone in while she went out to buy beer.

I love gardens. Other than, obviously, the spiders that lurk within them. That day, I'd been mowing the lawn (I am a really good friend and I also *love* mowing the lawn) and decided to go back into the house. Suddenly, I noticed a spider staring at me from my side of the fence. The pathway was too narrow to pass her without being in danger, so I couldn't get back to the house. There was nobody else at home - no friend, no housemates, no neighbours and no phone to call the police. It was just me, alone with the spider. The perfect day to face my fear!

"Fear is stupid. So are regrets!"

Here we go! Marilyn Monroe's quote was singing in my head. I'm not sure why it was singing. I think the quote merged into the Édith Piaf song: "Non, je ne regrette rien"[12]. I was ready to face my fear, free myself and live a new life - in liberty and peace. I took a deep breath and was ready to take the first step towards the big change I was waiting for.

I made a plan (I never make plans). But for *that* undertaking, I thought I needed one. The plan was to

---

[12] Which means: "No, I don't regret anything"

remove the spider with a branch and to throw the branch, with her on it, into the neighbour's garden. (Spiders are always female to me. I think it's because some species cannibalise their men, so I reckon there must be more *women* spiders out there. Moreover, in German we call them "die Spinne", which is female too, probably for the same reason). I measured and calculated and figured out that it would be best to walk backwards because, otherwise, if there was a breeze, the spider might blow into my face. I counted four steps to the fence and rehearsed the throw until it was perfect. I think I must have thrown over twenty branches into the neighbour's garden – literally stripped a tree – but, by then, I knew how to throw at the right speed and perfect angle. I was ready. Filled with blind panic, my knees started to shake, my breathing became heavy and my hands got sweaty. Marilyn Monroe started singing Édith Piaf again. I counted down from three. Then I counted again. And then I counted down from four. And then from three again. Marilyn got bored.

Then I said: "One", twice, and did it – I pushed a branch towards the spider's web, trying to capture her. It worked. I did it! I was holding a real spider on a branch, in my hand, only 20 inches away from my body. Time was suddenly speeding up, and so was the spider. I moved backwards, forgot to count the steps, stumbled over the lawnmower cable. Where the hell was the lawnmower cable in my rehearsal?! The branch with the spider on it twisted towards me. Turning my body while keeping my eyes on her, I stepped backwards, fell over the lawnmower and threw the branch away from me, which hit the fence and bounced back towards me. I tried to run away, somersaulted over the lawnmower and lost sight of the spider. There was a moment of silence. Marilyn stopped singing.

While I was holding my breath, I tried to locate the spider: in the air, on my clothes, in my hair. I couldn't see her. I totally panicked, ripped off all my clothes until I was completely naked, bent over and shook my hair as wildly as I could (I really hope nobody was filming that) and ran, screaming and stark naked, into the house. There, I jumped into the shower where I cried and sobbed and showered until my friend's housemate appeared from nowhere and asked if I was okay. Where did he suddenly come from and where was my friend when I needed her? After I'd finished my shower and washed off the fear on my skin, I diluted the panic I still felt inside with a lot of beer and wine.

What was the outcome of facing my fear? A grazed elbow, a huge bruise on my bottom, probably two years lost from my life expectancy, and I'm still terrified of spiders.

It made me re-think the whole concept of 'facing your fear', and I realised maybe it's best *not* to face your fear. I mean, I could've died falling over that lawnmower. Imagine if I'd accidentally hit the 'on' button, thus cutting off my leg, while I was falling backwards. It would have ended badly. And, if that wasn't bad enough, I probably really did kill a tree by using all its branches in my rehearsal. Now I feel guilty, as if I also played a part in destroying the rainforest and took away trees from orangutan families in Croydon.

Besides, thinking about people who have faced their fear, it never actually ends well. Never. Think of any horror film you've ever seen. Everyone who is facing their fear dies. When you are scared – don't open the door. When you hear an unfamiliar noise in the basement – don't go down there. Every protagonist who faces their fear doesn't survive. Don't do it! Don't look your fear in the eye. Don't be a deer and stand still in panic while looking at an accelerating car.

I have talked with a few people who've tried to persuade me to undergo exposure therapy. This is where you get up close and personal with something you're scared of. You give the spider a name, look at her, touch her, talk to her, make friends with her. You basically make something ugly, beautiful. How can that work? Let's think about it. For example: what if I'm afraid of thieves? If I felt that man stealing my backpack, should I have just turned around and said: "Oh, hi! How are you? I'm Alice. You want to take my backpack? Great... I also love the knife in your hand. And your tattoo is really adorable. Do you want to hug it out?"

Making scary situations cute doesn't help. Giving scary things names or touching them doesn't change them. They are still scary! Save the money you'd have spent on fear therapy and spend it instead on a new iPhone 11 Pro. Unless you're trypophobic. Then go for Huawei. But stay away from me.

I've concluded that fear is good. Don't face it, just call 999 or 911 or 133 or even 0044 911... depending on where you are. Or your mother, if it's about a spider. I've also found that a vacuum cleaner is rather helpful in spider-related matters when you're alone. The only issue is that they climb out of the vacuum cleaner at night. So, every time I vacuum a spider, I throw my vacuum cleaner out. Which means that every spider costs me about £200, which is expensive, but safe.

I think we should embrace our fears and see the good in them. My fear, for example, is good for Hoover vacuum cleaners. Other fears profit insurance companies hugely. We, with our fears, help the economy to grow and *that* is something to be proud of. So, be fearless about having fears, they serve a purpose because you will stay alive (although you might die earlier) and they increase your country's GDP.

TIME
MANAGEMENT

11. MANAGE YOUR TIME MANAGEMENT

Sleep less and go to the loo while sitting in traffic.

Time management is the ability to do something more efficiently, effectively and economically. It means getting more things done in less time with the effect of not being so stressed anymore, even though it will be stressful to work faster.

When you think of time management, suddenly everything becomes a waste of time. Who wants to sleep for twenty-six years of their life, wait in queues for five years altogether, and spend a whopping ninety-two days on the toilet?

Apparently, we spend roughly six months of our lives just waiting at traffic lights. The average American will spend forty-two hours sitting in traffic every year. I am not the average American. I'm not even American and I don't drive every day – but forty-two hours a year! What?!

When I read these numbers, I got stressed. I couldn't even check my own time management to analyse how I spend most of my time because I worried that I'd lose even more time by logging my time. I simply couldn't afford to waste time, particularly on time management. Every minute counts and I wanted to spend them – ahem! – on what exactly?

How do we want to spend the time that we save? By going to bed late and waking up early I might be able to retrieve some of the years I've lost sleeping. But what do I do with those extra years, besides being exhausted? In the few days when I've gained some extra time, by sleeping less and staying awake more, I sat around in panic, not knowing what to do with myself. Then I decided to go on Facebook and stalk 'friends' I don't even know. I also indulged in the food photos and happy couple pictures of neighbours I'd ignored in the street. Or queue-jumped in the supermarket because I didn't have time to watch somebody take their punnet of strawberries out of their shopping basket *really slowly* and put it on the conveyor belt at the checkout *even more slowly*. If my impatience didn't rip me apart from the inside, I would fall asleep while watching this boring display of inefficiency. I can't bear it, so I try to jump the queue to save five minutes of my life along with my sanity.

However, if the food they buy is then made into a nice meal and posted on Facebook it's a completely different matter. If my neighbour poses with her partner on a Friday night in their living room, toasting with a large glass of red wine and some flowers in the background then, *yes*, I'm interested in going through their photos for hours: snooping into their private lives, looking up their cat Phillipa – what a name for a cat! – who has her own album with some videos of her watching TV. Somehow, I ended up at their last holiday in Florida and realised that must have been with her ex-partner, as it was not the same woman she was holding hands with on the beach drinking a strawberry margarita. I ended up looking through the photos of the ex of someone I don't know, piecing together a story that I couldn't understand. When did they break up and why? What happened to their house in Kent and does this woman only date people who like strawberries? Hours later I found myself on the page of the ex's ex. I was emotionally involved and had seen the bedroom, the new coffee machine, and photos of a stranger's kids growing up. I was glad I queue-jumped because I gained five minutes – that, at least, compensated for this four-day Facebook detour.

Going back to the awfulness of life, there is another thing we spend a lot of time on: grieving. Grieving takes time. You get over break-ups and deaths and other sadnesses by taking time to grieve. Fair enough. But how many hours, days or years is enough? Do we even have time to grieve in our hectic lives? Looking at the time management spreadsheet that I haven't compiled, I already know that I don't. And I've just grieved for four whole months. Another time, I grieved for an entire year. Looking at my statistical projection, so far, I've grieved for 3.5 years – that's nearly ten percent of my life. Grieving! This doesn't include general sadnesses, frustration and depression, which take up even more time. I immediately reassign my allotted grieving time. And what if I also cut out unnecessary things like Netflix, social media and commuting? Keep visits to the toilet as short as possible, power-brush my teeth and stop making my bed (although making my bed was the reason I went on a second date with myself)? Still there remains the question: what to do with the time you win back?

Ever since I started to think about time management, I've been stressed out. Beyond stressed, truthfully. Life-threateningly stressed. I became the White Rabbit in *Alice in Wonderland*. Totally overstretched, never at ease. I'd have died in *Through the Looking-Glass: And What Alice Found There*. I became a bad, unfriendly person, started hanging up on people and stopped texting back.

Also, most of the tips for time management are inconsistent. One person says: "Do one thing at a time, get into it, indulge yourself and do it properly". Others say: "Do as much as possible – literally everything – but only for five minutes". Set yourself deadlines but go with the flow? Follow the rules but find your own way? I was so confused. Where should I start and why was I still sitting on the toilet?! Do what you like and quit making excuses? What was that about? Normally, I only make excuses for not doing the things that I *don't* like. Where would my excuses for doing the things that I *do* like come from? And did I *really* like these things? Instead of believing in myself and taking immediate action, I was questioning myself and procrastinating. I also read about the five-second rule[13]. How did five minutes get reduced to five seconds? I felt even more stressed, wanted to meditate but couldn't because if I did that every day for just ten minutes I'd waste over sixty hours per year doing it. Paralysed, I was counting down from five to kick-start my activation energy, but my reaction path was still linked to procrastination and I was looking out of the window thinking about ordering vegetarian duck dumplings and the new coffee machine that the woman in Kent had. Then, minutes later, an hour had passed, and I found myself back on Facebook again. How did that happen?

---

[13] Which is not the five-second rule for picking up food from the floor. It is the five-second rule for time management which says: "If you don't move within five seconds, your brain will kill the idea and you'll talk yourself out of doing it". (Mel Robbins, Melrobbins.com, https://melrobbins.com/the-5-second-rule, accessed 11 Oct. 2021).

This is another thing about time – sometimes a minute feels like an hour and an hour feels like a minute. How should I deal with that? "Time flies when you're having fun", as they say. But can I make the fun times pass slower and last longer, while making the tedious times pass more quickly and getting them over and done with? I was too exhausted to look up any other stressful suggestions disguised as good advice.

What is my conclusion on time management? Throw it overboard. It's the only way to keep the ship from sinking. Common sense is the best time manager. Depriving myself of Netflix is not the solution when I'm halfway through a series that I really like, which keeps me thinking and laughing. And if Netflix has bought my sitcom, you should definitely watch it too. Don't stop or reduce your Netflix intake right now.

I do agree that a constant wave of messages rips apart your focus when you're attempting to do something properly. Therefore, it's good to turn your phone off. Even if somebody dies and you weren't available to save them. It's very sad, but at least you got your task finished.

I also think we should multitask the things we don't like. In the minute that feels like an hour, or that endless, boring Zoom meeting: go on Facebook, Google your partner's exes, cut your toenails or text back your mother.

Don't waste your time during your time that *has* to be wasted. Grieve for as long as you need to, but try combining it with other tasks: grieve when you go to the toilet, or while you're sleeping. Grieve when your plane is delayed, when cleaning your house or filing your tax return. Combine it with other things that you don't like and get them out of the way together.

Time management is a lot like reading a beauty magazine. When you read a beauty magazine you don't feel beautiful. Regardless of how beautiful you actually are, you can't win against airbrushed perfection. There will always be the hair on your chin or the wrinkle under your eye, the dry hands and the fat roll on your hip – on just one hip, even weirder. Likewise, if I try to follow the rules of time management in the hope of being perfect, I'm less organised and more stressed. So, drop the literature and use common sense. My only advice on time management is give it importance but don't take it too seriously.

ORDER from

THE UNIVERSE

12. ORDER FROM THE UNIVERSE

Online shopping for dreams. Make sure to read the return policy.

Cosmic ordering is positive thinking with the ability to order from the stars. The universe doesn't accept dollars or bitcoin, it trades only in positive thoughts. It's like Christmas but the whole year round and you don't have to believe in Santa Claus or God, just in Google Books.

Create the life you desire. Thanks to the Law of Attraction and the manifestation of dreams you can get – and become – all you have ever wished for via the online booking system of the universe. After working so hard on yourself you can finally sit back, ask for whatever you desire, and let the cosmos do the rest.

This promise not only sounds amazing, it makes me question why I tried to work so hard on myself in the first place. Why did I not simply order a career, a lot of money and some self-esteem? Why did I go swimming, spinning and singing and not just sit on the couch with my iPad perusing the online shopping brochure of outer space? This advice almost came too late! I'd reflected and analysed, dated myself and played with my inner child, and *now* I was told that I could've just ordered a new girlfriend? Why not before?

Other questions hit my thoughts: Was it ethical? Or was it a bit like a mail order bride? Should I feel guilty even eyeing up the possibility? On the other hand, weren't there lots of other things that were immoral but economically justifiable? We all buy t-shirts for less than £5 and, in doing so, silently support child labour and inhumane working conditions in big factories in Bangladesh where workers stitch 'cry for help' labels into the backs of trousers. Don't we all read these articles and think to ourselves: "Something must be done!" then buy another pair of cheap jeans less than a month after the story goes viral?

Why should we assume that the universe has more moral standards than Primark? Who says that it bakes its cakes using organic, free-range eggs? We don't know enough about the universe to know exactly where our delivery is coming from. It has to serve 7.8 billion people (and that's only planet Earth). It is arguably more likely that it would use battery farm eggs.

I've read a few books on 'How to order from the universe'. Despite it sounding amazing, it was not so easy. I ordered a new backpack from the universe and waited for three months – it didn't come. I ordered it on Amazon – it came the next day. Then I read up on it more – the universe, not Amazon (I didn't want to look into the moral costs of my Prime membership). For the universe there are 'ordering rules'. Quite a few. There are a lot of things that you can do wrong, and the rulebook gets thicker with every dream that has not been delivered. This basically means that if your order does not arrive, *you* did something wrong. It's *your* fault; never the universe's fault. *You* asked wrongly. That is made clear in every book written by an enlightened universe expert as well as in the Bible (James, 4:3).

There is no catalogue that you can order from – you have to get to grips with it yourself. You can't order success, a nicer body or a stable job. But you *can* order a parking space, a partner and a parsnip (don't ask, it's a higher power, it doesn't have to make sense). You can't order money, but you *can* order ten pounds. The parking space will come to you, but sometimes not until the next day, because too many people ordered one before you did. The system is 'first come, first served'. As for the ten pounds – it might come as a five-pound note, a couple of two-pound coins and the rest in pennies the following week. You never know.

You must be clear when you order. The clearer the better. But this is not discussed in the language of the universe, which I assume is English. Or, if we go by population size, maybe Chinese. And you have to say "please" and "thank you". Be polite. The universe is quite British – even though it may not speak English – and appreciates manners. It's free, so yeah, at least say: "Thank you". Also be specific. That might be the same as being clear, but it gets another bullet point in the rulebook. If your order doesn't show up on the first attempt, order it again. Be even more thankful. If you get something different to what you asked for, it's okay. It was deliberate. That contrast between your order and your delivery shows you what you *really* want. You just didn't know it before. The universe did. It helped you out. And now it has shown you your real wish.

And don't argue with the universe, because the universe is always right. It's like a mob boss, or a priest, or a grandparent – just don't argue. It's said that it just wants what's best for you, so be open to it and discover what *is* best for you. You must believe that it is coming to you. As soon as you stop believing, the order will be cancelled. If you wait for ages and finally give up believing – cancelled. Yep, it's strict. If you receive £7.20 and stop believing – cancelled. Don't bother waiting for the remaining £2.80. It won't come – because you wobbled and started questioning.

And don't complain. If you do complain, the system won't work either. Be nice and humble. Because what you put out, the universe sends back. In addition, you need to practice. A lot. If you follow all these guidelines, your order will be sent. Have I repeated myself? Probably. Every rule is the same. They all sound like a load of whiffle (just avoiding using the word 'bullshit').

Here's another thing that irritates me a bit – I order books online, and films, but if I want clothes or shoes I go into a real shop to try them on. You never know if the trousers will fit, how your bottom will look in them or how high the waistband really is if you don't try them on. A picture won't tell you. A photoshopped model wearing them won't tell you either. And these are just clothes. How would it work if I ordered a new girlfriend from the universe? What will it send me, and how will my bottom look? That sounds like a recipe for disaster! Girlfriends are even more complicated than jeans – you can't just buy a new one and put the old one back in a box in the basement or donate her to a charity shop.

Also, the distances in the universe are humongous. Travelling to Pluto, the furthest planet – or not-planet, or dwarf planet, or planetGBT*... whatever Pluto is called now – from the Sun, takes nine to twelve years. Nine to twelve years is a bit vague. I guess it depends on traffic and loo breaks. Nevertheless, it is quite a long journey. And that is just in our solar system. The universe is much, much bigger than that. But let's imagine that I order from within our planetary system. If I order a new girlfriend now, she will arrive in twelve years. By then, I will be married with children and divorced twice. And I will probably have just started a new relationship with my ex's ex. Classic lesbian life. Also, I will be forty-nine! If the girlfriend I ordered comes from space, her time probably goes backwards. So, if she was thirty when I ordered her, then she will be eighteen in twelve years. That would make our age difference greater than her *actual* age! I am not a paedophile. I don't want to date someone that much younger than me.

I also think that the universe has no customer service. You don't have access to any reviews, and you're likely to support the 'big fish' by ordering from it. Yes, you don't have to pay when you order from the universe, but you do have to send out a lot of love and appreciation and you don't know who gets it. We don't know who its CEO is. What if it's a Putin or Trump? And you have spent years of your life sending deep loving waves and beliefs towards them. Awful. I don't trust it. It's not kosher. Every legitimate business has a record, a face of their company, and a website. Why should the universe be any different, just because it's based somewhere in the cosmos? You don't know what you'll get. You don't know if the products are new or used. And they're likely to be covered in cosmic dust so won't meet the WHO International Health Regulations. As a side note – don't order any food. It will be expired by the time it arrives and possibly create more chaos than a dead bat at a Chinese food market.

Of course, if it works for you – great. Continue with it. And, yes, maybe it does work, if you believe in it. Believing is giving something meaning. If you believe in something and something else happens, then you give meaning to that something else. And if you believe hard enough, you will make that something else fit the original meaning. Which makes you believe that it all happened because you wanted it to happen. As I said – great, if it works for you.

Maybe we should all try that, because it means everyone could be happy – if we all believe that we wanted what we got, and forgot about what we actually wanted in the first place. Retrofitting, basically. It's not about chasing your dreams; it's about *changing* your dreams. And that is probably the biggest spelling mistake ever made in the self-help books: chase versus change. Try as hard as you can to like what you get. And if you still don't like the jeans, the backpack or the new girlfriend, be proactive – just go out and try to find another one that makes your bottom look good.

Date
Others

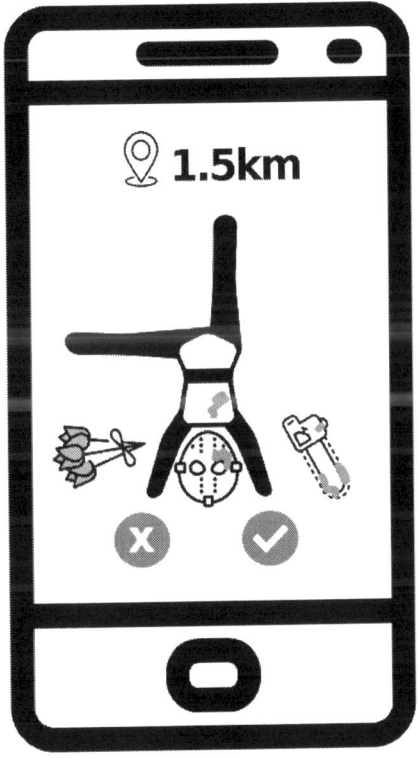

13. DATE OTHERS

To realise how amazing it is to be on your own.

Dating ~~yourself~~ *others is a social engagement* ~~on your own~~ *with another person, to assess whether you're a suitable prospective partner for* ~~yourself~~ *others to have a romantic relationship with.*

I reached a point on my journey of self-development where I was done with myself. Especially with dating myself. I didn't break-up with me, and was happy to be 'friends with benefits' for special occasions, but I was ready for new input. I found that spending days *by* yourself and your nights *with* yourself was *a lot* of yourself. Very intense. Almost too much. I am an actress and comedian; I needed (and need) attention and entertainment. I found myself quite repetitive. I couldn't cope anymore. Overwhelmed and bored, I wanted to swap my source of devotion.

I moved on to Tinder. Tinder UK not Tinder Austria this time. I had not been on Tinder properly for ages and it was very confusing. It had changed so much.

Everyone had a photo with a filter. What was that about? The filter made their faces look like a cat. With whiskers and cat ears. That was creepy! When I used online dating years ago, there were lots of photos of women *holding* cats. Now, they'd *become* the cat. Was that a lesbian thing? I was confused on all levels. What did these women expect me to do on the first date? Take them to a pet shop? Make sure to store Meow Mix in my cupboard? Was the whole cat filter thing meant to be cute, or was it verging towards bestiality? I was not sure, so I left-swiped all the cats.

But, honestly, the photos without any filters weren't much better. Everyone seemed to have photos with their friends. There were *four* women in one photo. And three in the next. Which one was my date, then? Or would I get them all? Could I choose? Should I write in the chat: "The second on the left, please"? On top of that, there was a lot of pouting going on. Pouting and half naked bodies. One girl was pouting and lifting up her t-shirt. In the background was her grandmother – knitting. I'll take the grandmother. She looked artsy and she clearly had good finger skills. Why not? Better than a cat!

Many girls were also doing handstands in their photos. Again, did I miss a trend? Why was everyone suddenly doing handstands in dating photos? Was it a new thing? Should you only date someone who can do a handstand? Should I learn how to do one myself? Would it make me look sporty, or flexible, or was it a sexual thing? Or did their phone camera just auto rotate so that they only *looked* as if they were upside down? Most of the handstand girls were in underwear. Maybe it *was* a sexual thing. Some were on the beach, but the majority were in their living rooms. One woman's handstand was on the beach wearing a bikini and boots with rainbow shoelaces. What was that about? Boots on a beach? She looked like she wanted to beat someone up after her handstand practice.

I ended up dating one of the handstands from the living room. Not because she looked sexy, but because she looked very unsteady. I wanted to make sure this woman was okay and still alive.

But Living Room Handstand Girl was weird. Who would have guessed? We went to a bar, had drinks until we heard the bell for last orders, and went home together. On the first date. But I guess I'd been dating myself for so long, I was used to bringing my date home. We had another three glasses of wine, which was probably too many. We started kissing and then she asked me: "Can you play some music?". I was in a panic and, suddenly, completely sober. The reality of dating caught up with me. Some *music*? *Music* for sex? Do people have a sex playlist? Was this a new thing too? I didn't know. I'd never requested music for sex. And I wasn't sure if it was a good idea. I have two nephews. My playlist consisted (and probably still consists) of 'Heads, Shoulders, Knees and Toes' and a bit of Cher. Because I love Cher. Actually, quite a lot of Cher. Neither of these seemed fitting for a sex playlist. Definitely not the nursery rhyme. And certainly not Cher's 'If I Could Turn Back Time' for the first kiss. Cher is amazing, but neither 'Believe' nor 'Strong Enough' or 'Gypsies, Tramps and Thieves' would've fitted for that kind of activity.

The only other playlist I had was filled with sad songs. It was actually called 'Sad Songs', devoted to my post-break-up life. Songs that literally made everyone cry. At the very first song Living Room Handstand Girl would have cried. I would have cried. Alexa would have cried. Maybe even the neighbours or the bus driver passing by the open window would have cried. I was not ready for a crying session with another person. Especially not on a first date. That was too quick, even for lesbians.

Under the pressure of having to select sex music from my limited playlist, I panicked even more. But then I remembered I had a subscription to a music app, so I could play anything at all. Living Room Handstand Girl left for the toilet. I calmed down and panicked again because I couldn't think of what to look for. I found a happy playlist. Happy? Was that a wise choice for sex? I didn't want Living Room Handstand Girl to get distracted and start dancing and singing. No. No happy songs.

I decided, there and then, that certain songs can't accompany sex. For British people one of them is 'Bohemian Rhapsody'. I've seen what British people do when this song starts. The sex would be over. Brits jump up, put a hand on their heart and shout as loudly as they can: "Mama, just killed a man!" *Nothing* will stop them. You can say something. You can turn off the light. You can even turn off the music. Literally everything you try will be too late after this song has started. Absolutely *nothing* can stop a Brit from becoming Freddie Mercury. They can't help scaramouch-ing and bismillah-ing until they end with "Nothing really matters to me". I didn't want to play this song because Living Room Handstand Girl would forget to have sex with me, or she would be too exhausted after the song, collapse and fall asleep.

By the time Living Room Handstand Girl came back from the toilet I was thinking maybe some classical music would be a good choice. Something like Beethoven, perhaps. It shouldn't be too relaxing – I didn't want Living Room Handstand Girl to fall asleep. But, similarly, it couldn't be too intense. Beethoven's Fifth' might be a bit too much. It begins with a "DaDaDa Daa!" that is very loud, very rich and very deep. And if we were just kissing when "DaDaDa Daa!" started playing, it would've felt wrong. We would have to be naked by then. It would be very tricky to get the timing right for classical music. I'd have to stop the kissing and the music, become Pina Bausch and talked to Living Room Handstand Girl in a choreographer's manner: "Okay, hold it right there! By the time we get to this part, we must be in our final positions! Don't delay at the beginning, go straight in, listen to the beat, the music comes in quickly! Once again! From the top! And: three, four..."

I decided – no classical music. No Beethoven. The best choice was probably club music. DJ songs don't have a lot of lyrics. And I didn't want lyrics to distract from the sex. If I played 'Like a Virgin', she might have asked: "Are you a virgin?". What would I say? "Ahem. No, I'm not. Or am I? I don't know. If you haven't had sex for five months, do you become a virgin again? Does it work backwards?" While I was still scrolling through my phone, Living Room Handstand Girl poured another drink and looked at me.

I took a deep breath and decided – DJ songs with only a few lyrics would do. Something like 'Barbra Streisand' by Duck Sauce. That would work. Two words, no confusion. Barbra Streisand can enter the bedroom. The more I thought about it, the more I was convinced that DJ songs were a good choice. I Googled a playlist from this famous DJ. It took me a few tries to find out that

his name was Fatboy Slim and not Fat-Slim Joe, but finally
– Living Room Handstand Girl liked it. We started kissing
and had a good time for three minutes. Then, thanks to
YouTube, we got interrupted by an advert:

*"Trouble hearing? Your struggle could soon be
over ..."*

I could not believe it! How did that happen? Not
only kitchen towel adverts, but now ads for hearing aids?
Had I really joined the target audience for that age group?
Completely embarrassed, I turned off YouTube.

Living Room Handstand Girl was okay with it but
asked me to do 'sex talk' instead. Sex talk? I can tell jokes,
but sex talk felt like walking through a minefield. How did
it work? Was it based on one-liners? Or was it more of a
storytelling thing? Were there act-outs or improv? Should
I do different voices and accents? She answered my last
question before I was able to ask any of them, when she
said that I should sex talk in German. I hoped that she'd
go to the toilet again to give me a chance to think. Sex talk
in German? I can tell you now that German is probably
the worst language for sex talk. French? Yes – French is
very sexy: "Voulez-vous coucher avec moi ... baguette?"[1014]
I don't know... something along those lines. Anything

---

[14] Which translates to: "Would you like to sleep with my ... baguette?"

really is sexy in French. Or Spanish: "Pela las patatas. Cortalas en rodajas."[15] That's a recipe for tortillas. Of course, that's all the Spanish I learned at school. But it is still sexy. German on the other hand, what would I say? "Ich möchte dich ans Bett fesseln und deine Brustwarzen küssen."[16] If you say that out loud it won't sound sexy, more like a quote from *Mein Kampf.* German is also a very literal language. For example, in English you say: "slippers" and in German you say: "house shoes". Or, in English you say: "gloves", in German you say: "hand shoes". A "kettle" is a "water cooker" and a "bra" is a "breast holder". Cute sometimes, but not when it comes to sex. The German word for "sex" is "Geschlechtsverkehr"; which, when you translate it into English literally means "gender traffic". That doesn't sound very sexy, it sounds as though I want to get involved in people trafficking. Maybe in English you'd say: "I want to kiss your nipples" – if that is something you'd say in sex talk, I don't know... But the word for "nipples" in German is "Brustwarzen"; which, translated into English, means "breast warts". "Do you want to have some gender traffic and I will kiss your breast warts and your shame lip?" (which means labia... yes, I know, I told you, it's not a sexy language!).

---

[15] This translates to: "Peel the potatoes. Cut them into slices."

[16] Which means: "I want to tie you to the bed and kiss your nipples."

It's not just a turn-off, it's a run away! I get really passionate on this topic as I did on that evening with Living Room Handstand Girl. I interrupted our romantic moment and gave her a lecture about the German language. She wasn't interested at all and said: "That's fine, do it in English then." In English? I learned English at school. I could write a letter of complaint. But sex talk? What would I say?

Aside from the fact that I didn't want to do sex talk myself, I also didn't want Living Room Handstand Girl – or anyone else – to do sex talk for me. First of all, I knew it would be very hard to understand her during sex. If she put a cork in her mouth and practiced pronunciation for twenty-five minutes beforehand then, maybe, yes. But, in general, no! During sex, everyone starts whispering and mumbling and dropping their 'p's, 't's and 'k's. It's impossible to understand what they're saying. One time, another Tinder date said to me, in the middle of sex: "Bab me." What does that mean, exactly? I said: "What was that?". And she repeated – in a sexy, but incomprehensible, voice – "Bab me". I couldn't even guess what it was. Could it have been: "Map me? Tap me? Mug me?" Did she want to steal my new laptop? Was I in bed with a thief? Or was it "slap me"? Maybe I do have trouble hearing. Google Ads is one step ahead of me! "Slap me" made the most sense to me – I thought it would be weird to tap her and couldn't imagine how to map her.

I also didn't want to assume that she wanted to mug me – we were half naked after all, it would take her a bit of time to get dressed and run away. I tried to find out one more time how I should "bab" her, but there are only so many times you can ask someone what they mean before you have to pretend that you understand. So, after asking her for the seventh time, I slapped her. It was very soft, as I'm not used to slapping people. This was definitely not what she meant. I didn't feel too bad about it, though. Maybe she has learned her lesson and will speak more clearly during sex talk with somebody in future.

Some people don't ask you for extras during sex but give you compliments, which I also don't feel comfortable with. It's a bit like getting a pep talk. They may say: "You're amazing", "You're so beautiful" or "You're great". This happened to me once and I was not happy. It felt too close to Louise Hay: a wonderful woman, but old and dead – I didn't want to think about her during sex. What's more, I don't know how to respond to compliments. If someone tells me: "I enjoyed last night. You are beautiful", I don't know what to do. Don't get me wrong, I like compliments. I love them. I want to hear them all day long. But what do you do with them? Do you return the compliment? Quickly think of what's great about the other person? Repeat what she said to you? Or pay for the next round of drinks?

Do you say: "Thank you", "Can I get you another drink?" or: "Is that all"?

I also didn't want Living Room Handstand Girl to ask me questions during sex. Especially the question: "What do you want?" What do I want? Really? I'll tell you what I want: I want a house, children, a career and a babysitter. I want to be paid for my work. I want to know if there is coffee in a turmeric latte. And I want to remember the password for my Apple ID. I want to live a life without struggles and spiders. And I want to be able to change the channel whenever I see ski jumping. These questions feel like the opening of a therapy session or a job interview. But not something you kick-start sex with.

And, while we're on it, another question I don't want to be asked is: "What are you thinking?" I have failed that during a date too because I replied honestly, which was probably not the best policy: "I am thinking about my debit card PIN." "Your debit card PIN?!" My date was very upset about my answer, so I tried to explain it further: "Yes, 4469." She got even more upset and said: "We are about to have sex and *you're* thinking about your debit card PIN?" I didn't think it was too bad. My debit card PIN is actually quite fitting for sex. If 69 is not the most sexual number, then I don't know what is. In the moment she asked me what I was thinking, I was actually debating with myself whether 44 was a sexy number as well, because then my whole bank card would be quite dirty. The night didn't end well.

So back to Living Room Handstand Girl, who was staring at me because I hadn't fulfilled her desire for me to sex talk in German. I decided if I wanted to get lucky, I'd need to up my game and just go for it. I could do sex talk in English if she wanted me to – it's all about intonation anyway. I cleared my throat, stroked her hair, kissed her neck and whispered in the most erotic voice possible some of my best English lines that I'd learned in school: "To whom it may concern. I am not satisfied with the service provided. I expected quicker delivery. Please improve your performance." Yeah, no, she didn't think that was funny.

Dating other people is a lot more difficult than dating yourself. Another human, another opinion, another preference and another perspective on the world. Everyone gets irritated, offended, turned on and off by different things. The only tool you have is communication which – "bab me" – can be more of an obstacle than a help.

For me, a first date feels like making tea for a British person. As soon as I put the kettle on, I panic. How long do you leave the teabag in? Do you put the milk in first? Cold milk or hot milk? Teabag out *before* or *after* the milk? Lots of milk or just a dash? Earl Grey or English Breakfast? It is so complicated. There seems to be no right but a lot of wrongs. You can upset people so easily by serving them tea. I never know what to do but at the same time I don't want to ask: "What do you want?".

What is the conclusion of going out, meeting and dating other people? Don't go for handstands, avoid cat-filtered people and left-swipe the ones holding knives in their profile pictures. They look scary for a reason. In the end, the big advantage of dating people – precisely *because* it's so complicated – is that you realise how amazing it is to be with yourself again. Alone with a cup of coffee and not having to worry about other people's feelings. If you want to be with other people though, be sure to let them make their own tea.

FOLLOW **YOUR** DREAMS

14. FOLLOW YOUR DREAMS

But don't go too fast.

A dream is a path full of obstacles which makes you become the person you want to be. It involves following something you love, which is hard work, tiring and expensive. But it is good to have a dream because Walt Disney said: "If you can dream it, you can do it."

My Grandma once said to me: "Some experiences you should experience for yourself, while other experiences should only be experienced by other people, who can then tell you about them." This was probably very wise advice, which I should have followed more often.

As a child, I always wanted to become everything when I grew up. I wanted to become a lawyer, a doctor, a pilot, a professional downhill skier. I wanted to be that person at a petrol station who puts petrol in the car. And I wanted to be the driver of that funny-looking water-splashing car with a lot of brushes that cleans the street. Everything looked fun to me.

At one point I realised that I didn't really want to *do* all these things – I just wanted to *be* them. To play them. I didn't want to study law and start my career in the basement of a shitty law firm, reading through boring cases of fence disputes between neighbours. No, I wanted to be Ally McBeal; a neurotic lawyer, defending people who get fired because of a bad hair day. I wanted passion, love affairs and big drama. I wanted to see babies dancing and share a unisex toilet with other lawyers who were equally bonkers. I also wanted to be an action movie star, a doctor and Batman one after the other. Like George Clooney. My mind was on fire – I could actually be a doctor without having to see real blood, defend people on death row without the threat of them really dying, and become a drug addict without taking any drugs. Fantastic! My dream took over – I wanted to be *an actress.*

My parents were not pleased to hear this. However, my mind was made up. I began my acting career with my sister in the basement. A lot of Austrian things start in the basement – sometimes good ones! We took our Dad's camera and spent hours shooting music videos, short films and commercials, accidentally deleting all the family holiday videos (or my parents' sex tapes ... who knows?!). I dressed up as Cher and Elvis and gave concerts in front of my mirror. I released my first comedy show, in front of myself, at the age of twelve, with a handmade toilet roll mic. This was then followed by lots of interviews with me, which preceded me nominating myself for an Oscar or two. My career had started!

I managed to get into acting school; but, since my parents thought I needed a proper education, I had to study business in parallel. Funnily enough, I learned more acting skills in my business classes than at acting school. I learned how to cry in front of professors, telling them that I only failed because I got confused about marking my crosses in the multiple-choice exams. I learned to pretend I knew things that I didn't, and I transformed every business theory I heard of into an acting technique. I conducted an expressive dance with my improv group to the 'Great Spurt' theory of Harvard University's Professor Alexander Gerschenkron. I also applied John Kotter's approach to change management to a concept for character development when I studied the role of Antigone, daughter of Oedipus in Greek mythology. And when I finally graduated from university, I didn't feel that I'd got a degree – it felt more like an acting prize for playing the best business student and this award was called an MBA.

I was ready and finally old enough to chase my big dream and become a Hollywood actress. Thinking that

Hollywood definitely needed another actress, I packed my bags and got a one-way ticket to LAX. I spent a year in Los Angeles, which was filled with a lot of things beyond my imagination. I met amazing people, I visited Universal Studios and the Warner Brothers studios, and I went to jail. Yes, I did it all. The last one was unintentional.

It started when I met my new friend, Jane. Jane had become an actress a few weeks before I met her. Her husband had quite a bit of money – he paid for her agent, her clothes and her boobs. I learned that this was the thing to do for a lot of people in Hollywood. Acting had nothing to do with reading plays and finding a voice or an understanding of the role you wanted to play. Acting was more connected to bleached teeth and a PR agent.

Jane was booked for red carpet events every night and did thousands of interviews there. She told me that showing up to afterparties and talking to the right people got her more jobs than auditions. One night, she invited me to join her on the red carpet. I was ecstatic. Hollywood *and* the red carpet – my dream was coming true.

It turned out to be anything but dreamy. I managed to find an outfit that I thought would fit and be *fitting*; but, sadly, compared to what I saw on the red carpet, I looked as if I'd made my clothes out of curtains – à la Maria von Trapp. Everyone showed a lot more skin than I did, so I decided to lose some clothes. But even without my cardigan I still looked Amish. I don't remember much of the event, just a lot of big boobs, big lips and high heels. There was Botox everywhere. And there was no-one with unbleached teeth. I didn't dare smile because I felt that my teeth were yellow in comparison. As the Austrian refugee, I was happy when the lights in the cinema went down and the movie started.

After the screening, I was desperate to go home, but Jane insisted that I stayed for the afterparty. I really didn't want to go so I said: "Yes, sure!" because, I remembered that this was the place where actors went to get jobs. This could be my big chance; *I couldn't miss it.* With my cardigan and yellow teeth, I got into my car and followed Jane. She was driving fast, in her Maserati. The traffic light signal was already changing to red. I didn't want to lose her and crossed the same light, but it was not changing anymore when I passed it. Seeing the flash of the traffic enforcement camera, I knew this would be a very expensive headshot of my car. And it was. $500 to be precise.

The afterparty didn't take place in a house in the Hollywood Hills, with a fancy pool in the living room. No, it was in the back room of a pizza place. I wanted a drink because I needed one. And, I thought, one drink would be safe if I stayed for a few hours before I drove back.

Sipping on my wine I started chatting with everyone, who all turned out to be actors and were disappointed that I wasn't a producer or director. About half an hour after we arrived, the restaurant closed. We had to leave. I was a bit irritated because I didn't want to drive so soon after having a drink. My first thought was to sit in the car and wait for an hour, but after ten minutes I was worried about getting carjacked. Instead, I convinced myself that it was legal to drive with one drink – although I knew I should probably not even drive when I was sober – so I made my way home. Just to clarify: I do have a driving license – an Austrian one. My Mother printed it and my cousin stamped it. But I am a good driver. I just sometimes confuse left and right. Which is very dangerous while driving. Or in political discussions.

Not long after I started my car I got pulled over by the police. Suddenly, worried that I looked drunk, my nerves made me appear to be even more drunk. I tried to lighten up the mood by being funny. The problem was that American police officers have no sense of humour. In Austria it's never a big deal when you get pulled over. The first question the officer asks you is: "Have you been drinking alcohol?" and the second question is: "Do you have any left?" I thought I could just joke a bit in the States, as I was used to this. The armed officer made me wind the window down and asked me: "Do you know why I pulled you over?" so I said: "Because of the dead body in the boot?" It was the oldest joke. Not even original! Clearly a joke. But he didn't laugh – not even a smile. Treating him as a standard comedy audience I thought I might get him with my next joke. He said: "Driver's license and registration!" to which I answered: "Yes, it should be here somewhere... It's not my car... I have stolen it... Joke!" This was also an old gag but, still, he was not laughing. It got worse when I reached for the glovebox to get out my driver's license. He suddenly put his hands on his gun belt and shouted: "Get out of the car!" I should have known from the movies that gloveboxes are usually where guns are stored! How could I have forgotten?

After a while, we established that I didn't own a gun and that my driver's license really was in the glovebox. Nevertheless, I'd lost the guy. He didn't trust me. I thought that everything that could have gone wrong had done by then, and that it couldn't possibly get any worse. However, it can *always* get worse.

A second officer was going around my car. I dared to ask what he was looking for. Officer Number One asked me to walk in a straight line. Then I had to touch my nose. I mastered each of these activities well. But then, for the grand finale, he asked me to close my eyes and count from thirty backwards. I'd never done this before and counting backwards from thirty was a bit confusing. I didn't know the purpose of this exercise but didn't dare ask this time, so I concluded that he needed to check that I didn't fall asleep when I closed my eyes. I needed to prove that I knew how long thirty seconds were – a timing exercise. I closed my eyes and counted. After having counted backwards from thirty in what I thought was exactly thirty seconds, I opened my eyes again. Delighted that I'd passed for sure, I smiled and said: "I am done counting!" Surprisingly, he didn't like that either. He got his handcuffs out, put them around my wrists and sat me down in his car. It would take me another month to find out what I'd done wrong. When I told Jane my story, she interrupted me and said: "Hold on a second, you counted silently?!" "Yes", I replied. "Of course, but I opened my eyes again in time!". She burst out laughing. Apparently, you should not count in your head which, having reflected on the situation, now makes complete sense to me. But at the time, there I was, in the middle of the street, with two police officers, and my eyes closed, counting backwards from thirty – in English – but silently. Now I can see why they thought I was completely hammered.

I did a blow test and, officially, was not drunk. But due to my behaviour – my silent counting especially – they decided to throw me in jail for couple of hours to make sure I was fit to drive again. I ended up in Van Nuys Jail, to be precise – apparently the worst in Hollywood. If I'd been arrested in Beverly Hills or West Hollywood, it would have been a five-star jail experience – and I could've met Paris Hilton or one of the Kardashians. But Van Nuys is a one-star jail: not the place to attract famous cellmates. While I was waiting to be put in my cell, a police officer went through my hair. Whatever she was looking for (drugs, weapons, lice) wasn't there, so she showed me where to go.

My cell was big: six beds, one toilet and a TV. The toilet didn't have walls, a door or toilet paper but, other than that, with the TV and air conditioning, it felt better than most Travelodges. I called my parents, but the officers had warned me to speak in English, not German, so I said: "Hi Mum, I'm in jail." She didn't understand and had to Google it. Then she said: "Oh, we're so proud of you!" I think she thought that I was in Yale.

During my night in jail, I made lots of new friends: a drug dealer, a prostitute, many wannabe actors and a director. It ended up being a really good networking experience after all. Better than the afterparty. The director cast me for her next short movie, and I gave her my frozen breakfast toast as a thank you. Sadly, I never saw her again. I'm not sure how long her sentence was, but I eventually went back to Austria.

By the time I left Los Angeles I'd never had my big breakthrough. I didn't become the next Austrian actress in Hollywood, or even the Governor of California. Nothing happened. The only thing that happened was my life in Austria became weird. People kept staring at me. Suddenly I was a refugee in my own country. Maybe it was because of my teeth. I ended up bleaching them so as not to stand out too much in L.A. But for Austrians that white smile looked really unnatural. I stopped smiling and started drinking a lot of tea to stain my teeth and look normal again.

After my year abroad, I didn't want to become a Hollywood actress anymore. I would if Kathryn Bigelow asks me to star in her next movie, though. I'd love to star in *The Hurt Locker 2*. So please call me if you read this. But, all in all, I was okay and ready to leave Hollywood.

After all these experiences, I actually disagree with my Grandma and think it is important to experience everything yourself. By everything, I mean mostly legal, of course. 'Chasing your dream' reminds me of finding a new hobby – it can be hard work and is not always enjoyable, plus it's often really expensive (it cost $3,000 to get out of jail after lawyers' fees etc.). And even if it was the biggest spelling mistake in history and the advice to 'chase your dream' actually meant to '*change* your dream', I think that you first need to chase it in order to change it later. So go for it. But perhaps get insurance – especially if your dream takes you to America.

DESIGN YOURSELF

15. DESIGN YOURSELF

Change your background and blur your wrinkles.

You have the power to design yourself anew every day. Make the change within yourself, so you don't need to blame others for your failures – even though it's their fault. Believe in yourself, then you will be unstoppable. But look right and left before you cross the street because the cars may not stop for you.

After a year of reading every self-help book available, I went to a bookshop and couldn't find a self-help book that I hadn't read. I have to admit, I was somewhat shocked by this. And the fact that I'd returned to buy yet another of these books made me realise that I was obsessed with them. This needed to stop. No more self-help books. I had to change my behaviour instead.

Returning home from the bookshop emptyhanded, I went online where www.verywellmind.com told me there are six stages of changing your behaviour: pre-contemplation, contemplation, preparation, action, maintenance and relapse. The only word I truly understood was 'relapse', but apparently relapse was not even part of the model if it was successful. I spent hours trying to understand the words behind behavioural change and, by then, wished that I could read a straightforward self-help book instead. Basically, behavioural change means: you think about thinking about it (pre-contemplation), you think about it (contemplation), you prepare for it (preparation), you do it (action), you keep doing it (maintenance) and then you relapse.

In my pre-contemplation stage, I found myself on YouTube. I needed practical guidance on how to get to the 'action' part and begin to change myself. I found a YouTube channel called 'change yourself'. A perfect fit! But after watching one video, more and more videos popped up and the topics were just too promising of a happier world and a better self to be able to ignore them. There was endless material covering every self-help topic, not just once but a thousand times. I was in self-help heaven. Motivational speeches, big-thinking advice, guided meditation, TED Talks, and my old friend: Louise Hay.

Since I still felt that I needed some help getting over a tough year, I spent seven days clicking through a variety of videos until I finally found a topic I wasn't familiar with: 'design yourself'. I was intrigued. I didn't know exactly what was meant by 'design yourself', but my closest experience of it was when I went shopping on a mission to give myself the makeover I deserved. I felt like I was starring in a makeover TV show, where you start by entering a shopping centre lost and insecure, and emerge transformed, stylish, happy – almost like a famous Instagram influencer. Goodbye old me. Hello new me. All my old clothes – the baggy t-shirts and skinny low-waist jeans – went to a charity shop and I conquered H&M. Ready to wear the latest fashion, I wanted to look cool and sexy, like Pink or Taylor Swift.

But my fantasy had raced ahead of reality. Stuck in the dressing room, I stared at myself wearing high-waisted jeans and short shirts with my belly hanging out. I looked like a grumpy forty year-old child whose parent had pulled up their trousers too high and sent them off to the playground again. No matter how many pairs of jeans I tried on, they all made me look awful. And what was the deal with the short tops that stop under your boobs, revealing half of your upper body? My poor, exposed back! I could get a kidney infection! I felt like a nagging grandmother, exited the dressing room and left all the clothes behind. I went straight back to the charity shop and bought my old jeans again.

Failing at revamping my clothes, I thought the next step would be to modernise something else – something external, like my flat. I read that changing your living space is good for the inner feng shui. It would not only be therapeutic but creative and would put a fresh spin on old patterns. That sounded good enough to me and easier than changing my fashion sense. Home alone, with Alexa playing Cher on a loop, I moved wardrobes, sofas and tables. One of the wardrobes in my bedroom was about three times bigger than me; but, full of determination, I thought that it wouldn't be a problem to move it on my own. My determination wasn't so strong when the wardrobe decided to tip towards me. In a panic, I pushed my arms against the wardrobe doors and my legs against my bed for some resistance. I ended up in a floating position between the bed and the wardrobe. If I'd been able to take a selfie, it would have looked really acrobatic – like one of those Cirque du Soleil performers. I've probably never been that close to death before and especially not for that long, because I spent hours spreading myself between the bed and the wardrobe.

Apart from the fact that I couldn't move, my front door was locked and my phone was in another room. I'd also not yet met my neighbours properly in person (only by stalking them on Facebook) so it didn't make sense to scream or shout or knock on the wall. While I was levitating, I could sense my muscles beginning to weaken. I could also foresee tomorrow morning's newspaper headline: "Comedian murdered by an IKEA PAX wardrobe, white, 175 x 58 x 201 centimetres." Would that be the most famous moment of my life? All the hard work, comedy gigs, writing, filming, editing and creating and I get my big newspaper article because I got crushed by a wardrobe? Or worse – what if I didn't get an article at all? What if my accident was not deemed interesting enough for the readers of the *Evening Standard*? Maybe they wouldn't even find me. A comedian not showing up to an unpaid gig is nothing special. People would probably think that I was an arrogant twat instead of dead, killed by a wardrobe.

In the end I didn't die, and I didn't have to go back into the closet. My shaking arms gave in, the IKEA PAX knocked me to the ground, but the bed happened to be my saviour and stopped PAX from falling onto me. They were both damaged in the end – broken and no longer useable. But I was completely unscathed. I didn't even break a fingernail. I'm a lesbian, I don't have long fingernails but even my short ones were fine.

Despite these two relapses in my 'action', I decided to delve deeper into the idea that you really can "design yourself". In particular, I wanted to know how it could be done without a near-death experience – or high-waisted jeans. So I was extra-intrigued when I spotted a YouTube channel that was actually titled 'design yourself'.

The videos were made by Emma – probably a twelve year-old vlogger – who was well-lit and came across as being very confident. She grabbed my attention by telling me that I could overcome my low self-confidence and design myself within the ten-minute duration of her video. She promised me tools and experience-based advice. I was an instant fan. What had happened to Emma? What was her backstory? Well, she basically didn't like her Instagram logo. And she constantly had the urge to change the font on her website. At first, it was difficult to understand what she meant, because I didn't know if my Instagram had a logo, and I couldn't even remember the font on my website. But then she told me how important a logo was, that it's all about first impressions and how you don't want to mess it up. It's important to communicate what you want and to show who you are. I looked at her logo. It was a light-green 'E' with a dark-green shadow. She wanted to change it to an emerald-green shadow, but was unsure whether it conveyed the wrong message about her. I still didn't understand and I've never thought about green so much. Emma looked straight into the camera and said: "If we eat at a friend's place, we are thankful for the food we get. But if we cook it ourselves, we are more critical." She was twelve and could cook already?! "We want to show people what we're capable of. We want to impress them", Emma continued. I was, indeed, impressed.

Emma concluded that it is okay to work hard and to deliver the best quality because our logo is the window to our soul and, therefore, we should not finish developing it until we are entirely happy with it. But sometimes we lose perspective by striving for perfection. She reminded her audience that we can change anything we've done at any time – because it isn't set in stone. But, in doing so, it's important to make sure that you're happy with your choice of green.

After listening to Emma talking at me for around ten minutes, I was baffled. She made me realise that the design comes from inside – it's our personal preference, it's what we like. And it's a battle. Behind every good design lies hard work, dedication and endless earlier attempts. Behind every change lies a lot of relapses. And that is okay, even for twelve year-old Emma and her choice of green.

I won't look self-confident or beautiful if I spend five minutes in H&M and dress in clothes that I don't like. I need to be happy with my choices. I need to find out what I like and continue searching for as long as it takes to discover my unique style. And one thing's for sure – I need a new font for my website.

FIND
A
ROLE MODEL

16. FIND A ROLE MODEL

Strive to be like someone you don't really know.

A role model is a person who is perceived by others as a good example. Someone who is worthy of being imitated because of their values, success or behaviour. This could be a teacher, a civil rights activist or a vegan.

On my self-help journey, so many of the exercises I tried were focused on me, myself and I. Therefore, I was unsure if a role model – an external influence – would be able to help me out of my misery. But then, I thought, maybe that's it. Maybe the solution lies outside of myself. Maybe I'd become a better, more successful and happier person if I strived to be like someone else and stopped focusing on me.

I went through my internal role model catalogue. My first role model was Ellen DeGeneres. Seeing Ellen, an actual lesbian *and* a comedian, on one of our two channels on Austrian TV, filled me with joy. So much joy that I bought lots of VHS tapes and recorded all five seasons of her 1994–1998 sitcom *Ellen*. This took me over five years because, in former times, we were not able to binge-watch everything on Netflix. We had to wait a week for the next episode and a year for another season.

Now, I'll officially be middle-aged in ten years' time, but Ellen still is a role model of mine. I've always thought she is great – I value her humour, her success and, of course, her lesbianism. Although, reading the news recently alleging a toxic work environment around her show suddenly made me question her as my choice of role model. Thinking about it, I realised that I didn't know her at all. I knew her sitcom character, her stand-up shows and all her jokes. And even though I've seen her talk show and every interview on YouTube, I don't actually know how she'd be if I invited her over for dinner. Would she arrive on time and take off her shoes when she came in? Does she wash her hands after going to the loo? Would she be honest if she didn't like the dinner, or discreetly spit it into a napkin? Not the whole dinner, but maybe a potato that wasn't cooked properly. Spitting food into a napkin was something I did when I was a child and my parents took me with them to their friends' for dinner. I remember one occasion when I really hated the food. I was too young to wash it down with a glass of wine and too polite to leave it on my plate, so I put it in my mouth, wiped my mouth with a napkin and let the food disappear into it – a trick I'd learned from my Mother at a young age. Always make sure that you have a napkin close by, in case you don't want to swallow disgusting food. It was a good trick and made me feel like a magician. Although, looking back, I must've gone through seven napkins, disposing of a whole plate of food. Maybe the hosts did notice the vast bulk of napkins that seemed to hide a whole chicken. Ever since then, I'm always wary of people leaving bulky napkins on their plate when I invite them over for dinner. I don't take it personally because I know I'm not a good cook, so it's normally me who leaves the bulky napkins on the plate at my dinner parties. Would Ellen do this too? Or how would she react if *I* didn't like *her* food? Is she a sensitive person? Would she cry? Would she kick me out or would she sue me? She's an American – Americans sue!

I felt the urge to learn more about her, to see if she was a good friend to her friends and, moreover, to revaluate if she was still a good role model for me. Google, as always, provided the answer. I found a website disclosing 'ten things we didn't know about Ellen'. After losing three hours of my day finding more websites like this (e.g., 'twenty-five things you didn't know about Ellen'), I finally learned two things that I hadn't known about her: she'd been a vacuum cleaner saleswoman and an oyster shucker. I had to look up the words 'oyster shucker'. It's a knife you can buy on Amazon. That left me with even more questions. I was not sure how to deal with this information. Would it alter my ambition to be more like her? I, for sure, didn't want to sell vacuum cleaners or to become a knife. But if I ended up with my own talk show as a result, I might consider it.

Since I couldn't make my mind up if Ellen was *the* role model, I started to search for what makes a good role model. Good values, exemplary behaviour and, of course, being relatable – these were the three top things. Jennifer Lawrence is said to be a great role model for girls because she knows what she wants, is down to earth and relatable. She's just like you and me. Even though she earned $46 million last year, according to the online science magazine www.hotactress.com. Michelle Obama is also said to be a great role model because she stands up for what she believes in, and she lived in the White House. This confused me even more. Should we strive to be like someone we'd never be able to emulate? Maybe I will earn $46 million if this book does well. It is possible! Michelle Obama earned $65 million with her book deal. I don't think she self-published, but our Twitter accounts have some similarities. She follows fifteen people and I have fifteen followers. That's a start. And, who knows, maybe I will find a new girlfriend who happens to be the next President of America and I, too, will move into the White House.

Of course, money isn't everything; but it's nicer to cry in the comfort and privacy of a taxi, than on the Tube while standing under another person's armpit. And if you have a slipped disc, a physiotherapy session costs £80, so it does help to be able to afford that instead of having to wait three (to thirty) months for a free NHS appointment. It's worse in the US, where my hypochondria forced me to visit a hospital. Five hundred dollars later, I was told that my bruise was not a blood clot and I would be fine. Later, I got another bill for $300, which was the doctor's bill. I got a hospital *and* a doctor's bill for checking on a bruise that I acquired from a drunken night out. I agree, money can't buy you happiness, but it does makes life easier – at least when it comes to hypochondria, parking tickets and an Apple addiction.

Elliot Page also popped up in my search for role models. He's an excellent choice – an actor, who's young career delivered astonishingly mature performances; and then, of course, when I was younger, she came out as a lesbian so she made it onto the front page of my 'role models' book back then. How could she not? Her touching coming-out speech at the Human Rights Campaign event, those eight minutes of emotion and tears, where every word she said had such an impact. I watched it over and over again. She became a hero for a lot of lesbians, not just for me – her voice, intention and bravery were inspiring and uplifting. I didn't learn the whole of her speech by heart – okay, I did, and I especially love this part:

"I'm here today because I am gay. And because... maybe I can make a difference. To help others have an easier and more hopeful time. Regardless, for me, I feel a personal obligation and a social responsibility. I also do it selfishly, because I am tired of hiding and I am tired of lying by omission. I suffered for years because I was scared to be out. My spirit suffered, my mental health suffered and my relationships suffered." [17]

Every lesbian I know loved that speech but then, when Elliot Page came out as trans a few years later it sent a shockwave through the lesbian community. Ellen became Elliot! Lesbians felt betrayed and sad that they'd lost their role model. I was quite happy because I already had one Ellen as a role model, and now having Elliot made it easier to distinguish them!

A role model can change, and if it is just their gender then great. But if it's a sex abuse scandal à la Harvey Weinstein – not so great. If their values are good and remain the same, it doesn't really matter if their haircut, gender or skin colour changes. Of course, there are not a lot of lesbian role models – far fewer than straight women role models. It would've been great if Beyoncé could have come out as trans instead, then, perhaps, we

---

[17] https://www.youtube.com/watch?v=1hlCEIUATzg

could have kept Ellen. But, maybe, we need more lesbians to come out. Also, just being a lesbian doesn't automatically make someone a good person. There are stupid and arrogant twat lesbians out there too. What made Ellen Page a role model were her values, which are the same as those that make Elliot Page a role model too. But why can't lesbians have trans, or other, role models? Can we look up to someone with a different skin colour, gender, sex and sexual orientation than our own? Can we have a role model that is radically different from us? For example, could Barack Obama be my role model? A black, straight man. Or could I choose twelve year-old Emma from her 'design yourself' YouTube channel? Can a role model be younger than me? Is that child labour? Or should our parents and neighbours be role models? In a small village in Germany, there was a father whose son wanted to wear a skirt. The boy's father allowed his son to do so, but everyone criticised his decision, finding it weird that a boy was wearing skirts. So, the dad decided to wear a skirt too and become a role model for his son. What a heart-warming story! I wished that my Mother had become a lesbian for me. Parents can be great role models, but the problem is they also ground you and make you do your homework.

The more I thought about role models, the more confused I became. To feel more grounded, I returned to thinking about me. I was straightforward. There were no surprises and there wouldn't be any surprises if I changed – I'd change with me. After doing some biased Google searches, I finally found a self-help article that suggested you should be your own role model. Your future self should be the one you strive to be today. Okay, I admit it – it was not an article, it was a quote by Matthew McConaughey when he won the 'Best Actor' Oscar. But while he was thanking his god, he used the words "God" and "scientific fact" in the same sentence, and I don't want to be inspired by someone who's done that. Nonetheless, the concept of being your own role model and shaping your future self based on the best version of who you are today is really positive and powerful. Therefore, I thought it would be better if I pretended this concept came from a self-help article and not Matthew McConaughey.

I was contemplating the possibility of making my future self my hero. But, thinking about it, my future self is probably an old, unemployed comedian, which doesn't sound too appealing – or heroic – to be honest. Then I had a brilliant idea: why should we restrict ourselves to humans as role models? Maybe it would be easier to choose an animal? What if I chose my neighbour's dog? She's a great dog – always happy, friendly and in good spirits; lives in the moment; and doesn't have an attachment or separation disorder! She's not a sex offender (although she did have that incident in the park with a poodle the other day) and all her needs are taken care of. Overall, this dog leads an amazing life, so I wouldn't mind being like her.

After all this reflection, I began to wonder, could I succeed without a role model? Could I survive hard times while chasing my dreams, without someone to look up to – someone who I could strive to be more like? While searching on Google on yet another occasion, I found a paper about the importance of role models. It said that a role model can actually change the performance of the individuals who follow them.[18] The authors had conducted a study with people participating in maths tests. When the test was handed out by a woman, who presented herself as being good at maths, the women in the test group achieved better results than in the comparison group, where the test was given out by a man. As well as the positive influence of role models, the authors of this research affirmed that people are at risk of conforming to the stereotypes of their social group. Something I probably needn't worry about if I strived to be a dog.

But I do agree with this study, and I'm convinced – being human – that these things matter and can be applied to other parts of society – such as in films. If a film has a

[18] Marx, D. M., & Roman, J. S. (2002). Female role models: Protecting women's math test performance. *Personality and Social Psychology Bulletin*, 28(9), 1183-1193.

strong female lead that isn't half-naked and saves the world, I feel like an action hero myself at the end of it. But if the movie I'm watching portrays women as weak (physically and emotionally), victims (sexually and psychologically) or dependent on men (socially and financially) then, of course, I walk home looking over my shoulder. When I hear footsteps behind me, I also hear Alfred Hitchcock's *Psycho* theme music and imagine that I'm going to be murdered within the next few minutes. I have a pulse of 160 and berate myself for not having written a will.

Naomi McDougall Jones is an actress and activist, and she recently gave a TED talk titled 'What it's like to be a woman in Hollywood'. In it, she states that female participation in archery went up 105 percent in the year that *Brave* and *The Hunger Games* came out. It's a start. Maybe, soon, there'll be an increase in female world leaders, corporate chief executives and top scientists, and the new iPhone might fit comfortably into women's hands and jeans pockets – or the jeans pockets will get bigger so they fit the iPhones!

All in all, I've concluded that role models are good. It's great to see how a famous person that I admire gets over a break-up and finds love again, comes out, or fights for human rights. It's inspiring. I also agree that role models can change, which means that it's okay to drop them. They may say something offensive, ignore their principles or turn out to be living a lie. Too many men I've looked up to have been accused of sex offences, which is incredibly disappointing[19].

In the end, *we* should be the change we want to see in the world. I think Mahatma Gandhi has probably said this already. We should keep our eyes and ears open, root out negative stereotypes and strive to change them. Maybe we need to be our own role models by being the best version of ourselves – putting aside time to be self-reflective, developing our strengths and skills, and moulding our moral character, all in the framework of who we want to be. Sounds like hard work, right? Then, maybe it'd be better to choose Google as a role model. It can find an inspirational person, quotation and answer for every situation in seconds. And it can find an archery course in your local area!

---

[19] R. Kelly, Harvey Weinstein, Keven Spacey, Woody Allen, Michael Jackson, Bill Cosby, Roman Polanski, Casey Affleck, Marilyn Manson, Alfred Hitchcock, Robert Knepper, Noel Clarke, Tez Ilyas ... to name just a few.

17. LIVE HEALTHILY

And sign up for organ donation.

Eat healthily, do plenty of exercise and sleep for eight hours a day. Or, maybe, a night – depending on your job. Living healthily decreases your risk of getting seriously ill. However, you can still get hit by a bus. And, at some point in your life, you're likely to die. But at least you'll die healthy.

Some studies suggest that a chemical in tomatoes called lycopene may reduce your overall risk of developing cancer. Does that mean if I eat a lot of tomatoes I won't get cancer? Other studies show that tomatoes absorb pesticides through their thin skins that have been linked to cancer. Do I now get more or less cancer by eating tomatoes? Is it better to stop drinking alcohol for a month and binge-drink for the rest of the year? Or would my liver prefer it if I drank only 2–3 units of alcohol per day? Would a diet make me feel better by cutting down on calories, or should reduce my intake of social media instead? Is a healthy body worth more than a healthy mind? Are vitamin pills good for you, or should you strive to nourish your body by absorbing all your essential nutrients from real food? Is skiing a healthy exercise or does it increase my chances of dying prematurely?

Veganuary, Dry January, Zumba and Vitamin D... but I could still die in a plane crash. There again, I don't agree with the principle of living every day as if it were my last either. Don't get me wrong, I think it's a great concept in theory – if it really *was* my last day. But, if I have to wake up the next morning, it's the worst idea ever. So, I try to live as healthily as possible. And the great thing is, there's so much information out there on how to do it. This means that we can filter our research according to the lifestyle we wish to follow, and only retain information that affirms our current values and attitudes! For instance, red wine lovers can quote from a plethora of research that red wine is good for the heart, instead of bad for the liver. A great confirmation bias! As a hypochondriac, I love Googling the symptoms of the illnesses that I'm convinced I have; and, in parallel, finding natural cures for them by eating more tomatoes or meditating. It all works quite well until I get seriously ill. Somehow, I'm only a hypochondriac of not-so-serious ailments.

From the age of nineteen onwards I've had a problem with my back. Over ten years, I've slipped a disc at least five times. But I've never thought of it as anything serious. I didn't want to do the exercises that my physiotherapist gave me – I thought it'd make more sense to run a marathon instead. This wasn't the smartest idea, nor was it much fun. I didn't even want to run a marathon in the first place – it just, sort of, happened by accident. But I did it. And now I can say that I've run a marathon and have a medal in a drawer somewhere to prove it; although it didn't help me to get a job and totally messed up my back.

The day before my Dad's 60th birthday, I woke up to catch a flight to Austria for the celebrations. I actually woke up *before* my alarm clock, but suddenly felt a shooting pain through my body. Every movement was agony. I leaned over the bed – the only position that was anywhere near bearable – and stood there for two hours without moving, watching the time when my plane should've taken off come and go. I took all the painkillers that were within reach, but nothing helped. I rang my Dad to tell him that I couldn't move and wouldn't make the flight. He didn't understand and said: "Just take a taxi." The idea of walking to the front door and sitting in a taxi was already beyond reality to me. Finally, I called 999, but the call handler said she couldn't dispatch an ambulance because I wasn't an emergency, which I understood – I wasn't dying of a heart attack, I just couldn't move. And, yes, by then I was even ready to pee on the carpet because I couldn't imagine walking to the toilet. I didn't know what to do. If an ambulance wouldn't pick me up, would I need to stand bent over the bed for six weeks before I was able to move again? The pain was unbearable, I couldn't think straight anymore and I'd run out of painkillers. I phoned for an ambulance again. The answer was the same: "Sorry, we can't pick you up because it's not an emergency". I asked the woman on the phone if it was an emergency if I slit my wrists. She said: "Yes." So, I said: "Be here in five minutes!". It took them an hour and a half to get to me but – finally – two big, strong paramedics arrived. Sadly, they couldn't carry me from my flat to the ambulance, though, because both of them had back issues.

Big Man One gave me a steal bottle with a mask attached and said: "Just take this and breathe in." I'm from Austria. If someone gives me a bottle of gas and says: "Breathe in" I get suspicious. I didn't want to do it. But Big Man Two said: "It's like being drunk." That helped. I took the bottle and inhaled as deeply as I could. It was better than wine. It was fantastic! I now take it with me to dinner parties. Nothing better than a veggie lasagne with a sip of laughing gas. Quite sweet in taste with a light finish.

After I'd finished the first bottle of nitrous oxide, I was able to straighten up from my ninety-degree position. Still in my pyjamas and without socks, it took me another hour and a second bottle of gas to walk out of the flat. I don't remember too much – I must have killed some brain cells with the laughing gas. But I know that I was in agony and kept crying because every movement caused a level of pain that I'd never experienced before.

In hospital, I didn't understand all the medical terms, so I said "yes" to every offer to reduce the pain and hoped that a Mexican drug cartel might provide something even stronger. The nurse asked: "Do you want an IV?" I didn't know that term in English, but I nodded and said: "YES!" Then I got a needle in my arm. It didn't help, so when she came back and asked: "Do you want acupuncture?" I said: "YES!" Again, I got needles – this time in my head. When that didn't help either she offered: "Do you want a suppository?" Again, with no clue what to expect, I said: "YES!" After that I stopped saying yes.

Pumped up on morphine and suppositories I managed to get to the airport. My Mother had booked me another ticket, as we were sure that I'd make it to my Dad's Birthday party the following day. At the airport, a tall young man who dealt with old people's requests, put me in a wheelchair and wheeled me into the business lounge. That was very kind of him, but it was a wasted effort on me because I couldn't wheel myself to the complimentary wine and snacks. Instead, I was left in the lounge for about an hour, watching other people getting drunk. Suddenly, a tannoy announcement said: "Flight to Vienna: final call". By this time, the morphine had slowly worn off and I realised that the tall young man had abandoned me in the lounge. I tried to stop people passing me with complimentary finger food to ask them for help as my plane was leaving soon. Someone finally pushed me over to the entrance where an airport car picked me up and drove me to the plane. With no intention to hurry though – I saw people with walking sticks passing us. Finally, after what felt like an age, I was the last person to board the plane. All the other passengers were waiting for me, and I could've died from the looks they gave me. By then, however, I was in so much pain that I couldn't care less what people thought of me.

The next day, instead of attending my Dad's party, I checked into the hospital where my journey of pain continued for another four months. From the outset, the doctor said that I needed surgery. But I said: "No, I can heal myself, thank you". Despite lying in bed 24/7 and counting the hours until I was allowed to take more painkillers, I still didn't believe that anything was seriously wrong with me. I thought I'd be fine. I was just a bit sensitive, but the pain would go away. I didn't sleep for weeks, if not months, and for much of the time was only able to lie on my side which then gave me a hip problem as well. But I read autobiographies of people who have healed themselves; I did reiki, affirmations and visualisations – still convinced that all would be good when I woke up the next day. It wasn't.

Months later, I saw my specialist again and she said that I had to undergo surgery. The nerve in my spine was so pinched that if I didn't have surgery soon I would lose bladder function. I was so scared of the surgery that I tried to see the positive in permanently wearing a catheter: "Sure, it would be a bit impractical, but I could binge-watch Netflix without loo breaks", I said to myself. But then, I thought maybe I should have the surgery and just swap the positive healing affirmations with positive surgery affirmations. The doctor was pleased. She said that she'd put me on the surgery list for the following day. A slot had become available because a patient of hers had passed away. I wasn't sure if she was trying to be funny or if it was actually true and was too scared to ask. The next day, *surgery day*, I told her that I was really scared. When she offered me another pre-med, I said: "I've already had three." She replied: "Me too!" and laughed. She reminded me of the pilot – I don't like funny pilots or funny doctors.

When I woke up from the surgery I realised that I'd survived! It'd gone very well – I was ninety percent pain-free, I hadn't lost the ability to walk and I didn't have to wear a catheter. Success! I was able to sit in the breakfast room and have breakfast with the other patients. It felt amazing to finally leave my bed; although, sitting in the breakfast room made me realise that it'd be another few months before I was fully recovered. An old man called Michael, who was sitting at the table next to me, dropped his knife on the floor. Suddenly, the whole breakfast room went quiet. All the patients there were on the neurological ward, and they'd either had back surgery or were waiting for one. Everyone pre-surgery couldn't physically pick up the knife and everyone post-surgery didn't want to bend down and risk their new, fixed vertebrae. It was an awkward moment. Thank goodness it was pre-Covid in 2020, so I was able to offer Michael my butter knife and ease the tension in the room. It took a while for me to function normally again – to pick up things from the floor and put on my socks. But I could finally live without counting the minutes until my next painkiller.

Living healthily is definitely a good concept – eat lots of washed tomatoes, go for walks and don't smoke (unless you find a good confirmation bias for it). Stay healthy, but don't get obsessed with it because you'll be more disappointed when you get ill, which is inevitable. And, if you get *really* ill, use self-healing thoughts but also use a medical specialist. It's okay to trust other people to help us out, especially with surgeries, as they are really hard to perform on our own. Live your life to the fullest, but remember you need to get up the next day.

STAY POSITIVE

18. STAY POSITIVE

Good things will happen. Maybe not to you, but they will happen.

Being positive is an ability to stay in touch with your feelings, being self-aware and accepting the things that you cannot change. It also means you have passed a test, are pregnant or have Covid-19.

On the topic of staying positive, I recently read that we think seventy-five thousand thoughts a day. I'd heard it before, but *seventy-five thousand*! That's a lot! I was as surprised as if I'd read it for the first time. I mean, I thought I talked a lot, but seventy-five thousand thoughts? That's just mad! What do we even think about in that number of thoughts per day? Are our ideas impressive? Revolutionary? Or just repetitive? Probably repetitive. Actually, repetitive. Yes, you're right, I think I've written this chapter already. But, on a good note, I'm finally repeating positive thoughts.

FIND THE FUN

19. FIND THE FUN

But get a flu jab and stop at the red light.

Fun is the lightness in a situation; the ability to express humour and laugh or be amused by something that has happened. Laughter is good for the environment and the people around you, unless you laugh about them. It leaves no carbon footprint, is free of charge and should be included in a balanced diet every day.

If I wrote a self-help book instead of an Anti Self-Help book, "finding the fun" would be my advice. My only advice. And it would be very short. Just this single chapter.

I have a childhood memory of my Mother being totally beside herself. She left the flat and ran downstairs, little five year-old me behind her. She was angry, shouting and in tears. I knew that the most horrible thing *ever* had just happened – I've forgotten what it was now – but, at the time, I was sure: the world was going to end. I had never seen my Mother cry before. I didn't even know that mums had tears. In that moment I was convinced that nothing would ever be okay again. Ever.

Then, about a week later – we were all still alive – my parents' friends came over. My Mother started to tell them the story of what had made her so upset the week before. My child-self felt as if the tornado was catching up again, as per Dorothy and Toto in *The Wizard of Oz*. This was the moment I'd been waiting for: the big showdown. Scared but prepared, I was looking out for the tornado, the millennium bug *and* Roland Emmerich entering our living room filmset, directing my Mother and ending the world with her tears. But then, something weird happened: my Mother started to laugh. No tears, just laughter. What?! Soon, she was laughing very hard and couldn't stop. Her friends were also holding their bellies in laughter. What was happening? There was I with scared eyes, bigger than my face, and my Mum was laughing her socks off. It didn't make any sense at all. A week ago, there was almost an apocalypse and now she was laughing? I was speechless! However, in that moment, I realised something very profound that has stayed with me ever since:

Awfulness + Time = Great Story

From a broken leg to back surgery or spending a night in an American jail to moving in with a lesbian porn director – all challenging situations, but now: great stories.

Yes, I did move in with a lesbian porn director when I was living in Los Angeles. She was not the film director I met in jail, who never called me back. This was a different woman, but she was in jail too. This story needs a whole new book, which goes way beyond my Anti Self-Help Book-not-book. It was a mad situation but is a *great* story. But I will say: I did watch all of her movies out of respect for her work, which was a challenge because when I see naked people on TV I normally look into their eyes... but in these kinds of films the eyes are not in frame anymore.

Anyway, I've lived with the formula "Awfulness + Time = Great Story" for a long time. Maybe it's why I became a comedian. Or, maybe, I became a comedian because I seem to experience a lot of mad things in my life and they're far easier to process with humour.

I was already working as a comedian before I bought my first book about how to write jokes, by James Mendrinos. My timing – as you may have noticed – is often terrible: I should have bought *The Complete Idiot's Guide to Comedy Writing* before I started working in comedy, but at least I was "original" for a few years. Nevertheless, in the book I discovered that there is such a thing as a joke formula:

Premise + Point of View + Twist = Joke

And not just James Mendrinos, there are many others who've published their own formulas, such as Judy Carter in *The NEW Comedy Bible: The Ultimate Guide to Writing and Performing Stand-Up Comedy*:

Attitude + Topic + Premise + Act Out = Joke

But probably my favourite description is from Tina Fey, who says:

> *"Comedy is truth, plus time, multiplied by monkeys, divided by one fart."* [20]

What all these quotations have in common is that you can find a joke, a climax and a punchline in *every* situation. Sometimes it's physical comedy when somebody falls into your sister's wedding cake or slips on a Fairtrade banana skin while wearing a Covid-19 face mask in the supermarket. Other times it's dark humour, which is observational and, often, self-deprecating. Whichever approach you take, there are endless possibilities to find the fun *in* or make fun *of* a situation. You have to push aside the obvious and see a new perspective to find the twist. A surprise. Something unexpected. Exaggeration, malapropisms, metaphors, sarcasm, satire, shock, spoonerisms – anything really. Don't ask me what half of these words mean because I don't know. I've copied them

---

[20] https://www.news.com.au/entertainment/celebrity-life/tina-fey-on-how-to-be-funny/news-story/dbf16526441088c3a572023b76508a6a

from a lecture that I was asked to give as part of a course at a London university called 'Comedy in the Community'. When I did it, I sounded confident even though I didn't really know what I was talking about. That's the difference between comedians and academics. Comedians don't know but pretend to know, academics do know but think they don't know. Dunning–Kruger Effect meets Imposter Syndrome.

A formulaic approach to comedy is a new thing to me. But finding the joke is something that has intrigued me ever since I was young. I'm almost obsessed with it. It's like twisting the Rubik's Cube of every situation until all the colours match. Searching for the joke happens mostly in inappropriate situations, though. You hear stories from comedians who interrupted their lovemaking to write down a joke. Or joking with a police officer after being pulled over – there's a good chance that all comedians have done that. There was even some humour on the day that my family sat around my Great-Grandma's deathbed. We were eating *Ildefonso* – an Austrian chocolate with an inspirational quote inside – the Austrian equivalent of a Chinese fortune cookie. One of the quotes said: "Change is happening in your life, so go with the flow!" It felt so absurd and inappropriate in that situation, that it made us laugh. And it seemed to affect my Great-Grandma's heart rate, which had lowered, but then came back up again with every new quote. She passed away that day after we stopped eating the chocolate. Although we were sitting around in sadness, some comedy had found us and made a difficult situation a little more bearable. It came naturally and connected us – almost as a necessity. And, I think, even though she was not conscious anymore, my Great-Grandma needed that last laugh too.

Not long after my break-up, I had a laugh as well. Just looking at my tearstained face in the mirror made me laugh because it looked so ridiculous. I always had hopes of a big acting career, and wished I had an attractive crying face rather than one that made me laugh. But it was rather helpful in that situation.

Moreover, laughter is really healthy. It doesn't heal the pain, but it makes you laugh through it and that, at least, gives you a higher pain tolerance. Laughter increases the blood flow, burns calories, reduces muscle tension and massages internal organs – whatever that means. Apparently, the body doesn't know the difference between a fake laugh and a real laugh. So, I've decided, next time someone breaks up with me, I will just start laughing. That should do the trick. I'll lose weight, relax and accept it, while enjoying the side benefit of an internal Thai massage.

Knowing the goodness of laughter, how can you incorporate it into your daily life? I think it's critical to be able to make fun of yourself. Make yourself important but don't take yourself too seriously. Have self-confidence but don't be arrogant. When you get attacked by someone – physically or verbally – think "*Aikido*". Aikido is a modern Japanese martial art that allows you to defend yourself while protecting your attacker from injury. A nice fight, basically. You achieve this by taking the energy from your attacker and redirecting it. So, if you get attacked by somebody, engage with it – take the initiative. When Abraham Lincoln was verbally attacked during the Lincoln-Douglas debates, when Douglas accused him of being two-faced, Lincoln deflected this criticism by saying:

"I leave it to my audience: If I had two faces, would I be wearing this one?" [21]

If you don't want to make fun of yourself, instead of getting angry and upset, make fun of the other person. If someone catcalls you – as happened to me the other week, when a man shouted: "Oooh, how much do you charge?" – don't get aggressive. Just have fun with it. Say what I said: "I don't charge money. I charge in brain cells, but you can't afford me." And then, maybe, run. As fast as you can. Because that comment is a bit more Karate than Aikido.

[21] https://www.saturdayeveningpost.com/2013/06/lincoln-jokes/

I also think humour helps others to understand you. To learn. When I came out to my Catholic Grandma, who said homosexuality is not natural, I simply answered: "Neither is your artificial hip. But you still sleep with it every night." She didn't understand because I was speaking English, but I felt better. And I'll probably still inherit something from her. Hopefully.

Humour is also great when you want to deliver an important message. Air New Zealand does an amazing job at communicating boring safety instructions to passengers in a fun and entertaining video, using Hobbits to draw attention to life jackets and emergency exits. I've never seen people – even cynical seasoned travellers – so interested in watching an airline safety video, from beginning to end.

Humour can be a great tool when you have to communicate a difficult message too. If you want a pay rise from your boss, need to explain bad medical results to a patient, or want to break up with someone: just think of a punchline. Try to package it as a joke. Try to make it as fun as possible. Use some dark humour, a bit of slapstick or Tina Fey's fart.

Recognising that bad situations are filled with fun and inspiration can actually change your life. Not necessarily for the better, but your life will undoubtedly be different. Like mine. I not only see great material in bad situations – I often feel that I'm actively looking for holes to fall into just to get more insights from it. Writing a new solo show represents a year of agony for me. Writing this book required a stolen backpack, a break-up and a coronavirus lockdown living with my parents. It's not pleasant, but it is productive and then the fun (or the funny) follows later. When there is an awful situation unfolding right in front of me, there's a little voice inside my head telling me: "Go there!", so I grab a pen and some paper and off I pop.

Maybe, if you're not a comedian – if you're a normal person who just wants a happy life – then you don't want to discover the inner voice that sends you towards the deepest misery. Fair enough. What I'm saying is simply that when something bad happens, don't try to think positively, just try to find the fun. Change your perspective and try to capitalise on the situation. You don't have to wait for the dust to settle – you can stand in the middle of the maelstrom and still have a laugh. You might not have a job or money or a relationship, but you'll have hours of fun. That is invaluable. In a currency that doesn't pay for your wine, nevertheless you can call yourself rich. And you can always write a book about your experiences and hope people buy it.

When I was in the American jail, and I finally told my Mother that I was in jail and not in Yale, she was shocked. As I've said, it's almost impossible to get arrested in Austria. When a friend of mine failed the sobriety test, the police took away his driving licence and said: "Come to the station tomorrow morning and pick it up" and let him drive home. For everyone who lives in Austria, it's a huge deal to get arrested. My Mum was upset and almost out of her mind when she found out about my night in jail. But I calmed her down and said: "Mum, give it a week, it'll be a great story." And it was. It was the main focus of my second one-woman show that I toured in Austria. Nobody came to watch it, but that is not the point.

You don't have to get arrested to find a joke. You could just have a shower. If you're bored or unhappy, go to the bathroom and look around. Ask yourself questions about everything you see there. Questions that Ellen DeGeneres asked herself. She wondered why there is a help hotline on the back of a shampoo bottle. Who'd call this number? And, worse, who'd actually work there? How would the conversation go? She turned this material into a brilliant stand-up routine that kept me entertained for years.

Comedy is not a cure, but it is healing. It doesn't make things better, but it does make them funnier. We can all do it. We don't need comedians to point out these things. I mean, you do, so please follow me on social media and come to see my shows. But if you're too depressed to leave the house, or have no money, you *can* do it yourself. Until you are better ... then don't forget to come to see my shows[22].

Last but not least, it's also good to remember that happiness isn't everything. Next time you desperately need the loo and finally find one – *just in time* – you'll realise: there's more to life than happiness – like toilets, for example.

---

[22] All info and gigs can be found at: www.alicefrick.com... If you don't see my face on that domain, I have not paid for it, so just Google 'Alice Frick'.

CONCLUSION

20. CONCLUSION

The beginning of all problems.

A conclusion is the end of an event, a closure or a decision reached through reasoning. It is the last comment of a speech, the grand finale of a play and the death of a spider. It's final. Unless it is an introduction.

While writing this book, I was making myself a coffee one Tuesday morning when I suddenly received a phone call. Suddenly? My phone doesn't normally ring. I get texts, but hardly ever calls. Unless it's my Grandma, who only calls on Sundays after church to ask me how my week was and if I've got married yet. So, my phone ringing on a Tuesday morning was a big surprise. This could've been a scam caller asking me if I was involved in a car accident, or the council telling me that I hadn't paid my council tax bill. I'd just taken the oat milk out of the fridge when my phone, on the table, started to vibrate. I jumped. Very suspiciously I picked up. It was a woman. Maria. She told me that she had my brand-new laptop. I spilt the oat milk because the lid wasn't on properly. "The thief?!" I shouted. The woman on the phone said: "Yes." I grabbed my absorbent, strong and durable kitchen roll and started to clean the sodden kitchen floor.

I was so shocked that she'd finally returned my call! After all these months. And even more shocked that the thief was a woman. I'd been stereotyping a poor, innocent man. No wonder some white, straight men think they're victims of discrimination. If even *I* - an oat-milk-drinking lesbian from Austria, with many friends from all over the world and across the gender spectrum - can impose unconscious bias and prejudice on people, then what hope do we have? Poor them! Although, in my mind, I'd never pictured the thief as a Caucasian male, but a stereotypical Mexican drug lord, called José, covered in tattoos, selling drugs when he wasn't stealing backpacks. And straight. Yes, he was straight and had a lot of one-night stands with good-looking women much younger than him.

Then, I felt awful for putting all men called José in that box of stereotypes, to the point where I was thinking of creating a charitable organisation to raise awareness that not all Josés are bad! We need to raise awareness that some women are also bad! Women called Maria! No doubt Maria was from Mexico too - a lesbian with short hair and a lot of tattoos. Convinced I was chatting to the thief, I told her it was too late - I'd changed the lock on my front door and didn't need the backup of my data anymore. She could keep my laptop.

It took me almost thirty minutes to realise that I was talking to *Officer* Maria, who had a Scottish accent, not a Spanish accent, and she was not the thief but had *found* the thief. Or the man the thief sold my laptop to. "So, the thief was a man?", I asked. "The person who wanted to sell your laptop was a man, so if you want to come to the station..." I had to interrupt her: "And do you know if the person who actually stole it was a man too?" Now she was confused that I wanted to discuss the gender of my thief, instead of asking for details about how to retrieve my laptop. My idea of the "not all Josés are bad" charitable organisation was postponed for now.

It took another hour – and three cups of coffee – before I was able to get a complete picture. There was this online resale company that got busted a couple of days after my laptop was stolen. The owner had a lot of stolen computers, cameras and camera lenses – about half a million pounds' worth – in his flat, a shithole in North London. He obviously didn't spend the money on a nice flat in the City to impress his parents. Officer Maria told me they had to empty a prison cell to store all the stolen goods they recovered. I'm not sure what they did with the criminals they evicted from that cell, but I'm glad my laptop had a bed for the night. Or, more accurately, *nights.*

Because it took the police over a year to sort out what belonged to whom and to call all the victims of the thefts. Somehow, I was last on the list. Later, I discovered that the actual thief in the coffee shop *was* a man. Two men, in fact. My idea of the "not all men are bad" charitable organisation was postponed too. Maria had seen CCTV footage of their crime. They were wearing hats, so you couldn't identify their faces. One of them walked by my table and kicked my backpack straight ahead; then, after he'd walked past, the other one bent down to grab it. I must admit, it was a clever manoeuvre. If I ever want to steal anything, I'll be sure to team up and wear a cap.

Maria, who took custody of my laptop, knew a lot about me – she knew I was a comedian; saw pictures of my ex and I wearing huge conical rice hats on our holiday in Vietnam the year before; and reminded me that it was my Dad's birthday, according to my Google calendar. She also congratulated me for running a marathon and thought it was a great achievement. Finally! So, it *was* worth it! I wasn't sure how she'd unearthed all these details – she must've figured out the password for my laptop. I guess I should change it from 'alice1' to 'alice2' next time. She added that she liked my jokes and asked me to come to the police station. I wasn't sure if she wanted me to give a statement or a stand-up comedy show.

I was dazed. First, I was obviously very flattered that Maria liked my jokes. Second, I couldn't believe that they'd found my laptop. After a whole year. In a city with more than nine million people and, probably, even more laptops. What were the odds? With this luck, I should start playing bingo and ordering from the universe again! Maybe, when I asked for a new backpack that didn't arrive, the universe returned my brand-new laptop instead. It wanted to show me that it's more important to ask for what's inside – instead of the outer shell. And it took months to be delivered because I stopped believing. Now it's arrived, I can believe again! Perhaps, it works after all. I should definitely order a new girlfriend next.

Although I was truly amazed that my laptop had been found, I didn't want it back. I genuinely didn't. All this time I'd been thinking about it. Missing it. Wishing it back. Trying to make sense of it. Playing a film of the event inside my head, over and over again. Who'd taken it? What was that person doing with it? Would they laugh at my jokes, but in a bad way? Would they sift through my keepsakes and criticise my photos? Why wasn't I more vigilant? How did I let it happen? Was it all my fault? What could I have done differently? Every "What if...?" question out there had eaten me up for weeks on end. After months of misery and grieving, I'd *finally* given up. I accepted the situation, moved on and reconciled myself with a new laptop. I was happy. I finished this book, wrote

247

new jokes and felt Yin and Yang in my heart again. And now this? I stared at the fruit flies as they waggle-danced around the brown banana I was about to slice into my breakfast muesli.

When Maria phoned, I'd had no contact with my old laptop for a whole year. One. Whole. Year. It'd been hard work, but I'd let it go. Made a clean break. And now she was asking me to take it back? Furthermore, it was *her* who'd gone through my jokes, not the *thief.* And there was not just one thief. There were three thieves! Everything I'd imagined was different – I didn't know if it was better or worse, but I just couldn't bear the thought of taking it back. What would I do with it? Compare it to my new laptop and my new holiday photos? Stare at the nostalgic desktop screensaver? Blame myself for not waiting a few more months before buying a new one? Berate myself for not resorting to handwriting, just in case I got my old laptop back? I didn't want to do that. Any of it. I'd moved on. I'd made peace with the one I'd lost, restored the data I needed and chosen a different screensaver. I didn't want to feel guilty. Having to pick up my old laptop made me really upset. And this 'upset-ness' made me feel even more upset because I thought I'd moved on and, suddenly, I wasn't sure that I had. "It's just a laptop", Maria interrupted.

Losses and break-up pains remind me of a slipped disc. It's truly awful. Not just the awfulness of the moment the disc slips, but also the knowledge of how long it will take to heal. One second in the shower, you twist to grab the shampoo, amusing yourself with the thought of calling the helpline number on the back of the bottle ... and, suddenly, indescribable agony. Life changes in a single second. I normally cry when it happens – not just because of the pain, but because I know it will be *months* before I'm able to dress myself again. *Everything* will slow down. I will have to cancel gigs, parties and football. And I won't be playing a racoon for a long time.

Maybe Abraham Maslow was right after all. Previously, I'd tried to turn his theoretical hierarchy of needs into an upside-down cocktail glass. But maybe, I should agree with him. Maybe we should take care of ourselves by attending to the bottom of the pyramid. Maybe we should think of food, water, sex and sleep first instead of aiming for the peak of self-actualization.

Maybe after a horrendous experience we don't need to start looking for our self-respect, self-confidence and our favourite pair of socks, but should prioritise nice dinners, a comfortable bed and sex. Maybe we should slowly build everything up again and not expect the top of the pyramid to shine, when the bottom is unstable. Any old socks will warm our toes and stop our shoes from rubbing on the way.

The hard thing is that a lost possession or person haunts our thoughts for a long time. She/he/it becomes a ghost – a fantasy or virtual reality without the expensive goggles. Then, when we're suddenly confronted with it in real life, we often realise that we don't need it anymore. And we don't want to take it back because it was painful to let it go.

When Maria hung up, I realised that not only:

$$Awfulness + Time = Great\ Story$$

But also:
$$Awfulness + Time = Healing$$

It is, of course, not that simple because there are other forces like toxic relationships, idiots and gravity. These things don't alter with time, but for an Anti Self-Help Book of nearly 250 pages, I found this was a good enough conclusion.

After I'd finished my new formula, I went to the police station. After all, Maria was right – it was only a laptop. While I signed the paperwork and gave a statement – not a comedy show – I had a feeling that I knew Maria. She didn't have tattoos and short hair, like I'd imagined she'd have when I thought she was my thief. But I still thought she looked familiar. I was convinced that I'd seen her before and thought maybe she was the police officer who'd pulled me over because I was speeding. Was she the one who didn't want to take a selfie with me so I could sell it on social media? Maria smiled, shook her head and said: "No. I've not pulled you over – yet." I'm not quite sure what the "yet" meant. I kneeled to put the laptop in my bag and saw Maria's shoes – black boots with rainbow shoelaces. Suddenly it hit me: I *did* know her! She was Beach Handstand Girl on Tinder! I looked up at her face. Maria smiled at me. She was cute but my handstand alarm bells were ringing. I smiled back and ran out of the station. I forgot my jacket, so I had to go back for it and then I ran out again.

As for the laptop, I decided to wipe all my data (after I'd backed it up again ... and again ... and again) and give it to my Mother. She was delighted by this surprise. I mean, she still doesn't know how to use it, and will never fill up two terabytes of memory; but she can FaceTime me now and can see my head in life size.

My conclusion is that you don't have to let your past restrict you. If your ex wants you back, hook her up with your mother. No, don't do that – unless your mother doesn't mind. You can literally reinvent yourself every single day. Get a new website and be your own role model. It's all about learning to see change as a chance, rather than as an obstacle.

A great inspiration for me is a comedian friend of mine. She started comedy when she was over seventy years old. When she turned eighty-seven she began looking into funding for her PhD; as well as finding a new flat, she also wanted to adopt a dog. This made me realise that most of the restrictions we put upon ourselves are limitations that our problem doesn't even have. We can change ourselves and the purpose of our laptops – any time we like.

If you are as impatient as I am – and want to see the change happening as soon as you think about it – always remember that change is a process, not a moment. Unless you get hit by a bus. Then change is a moment. Don't get hit by a bus, first look right when you cross a road in the UK. Then look left, then right again – especially if you're from a country that drives on the opposite side of the road. It's really dangerous. And if you sometimes confuse left and right, like I do, then don't risk crossing the street at all.

Coming to the end of this book, if you're asking yourself what you can take away from all this anti self-help advice, I'll sum it up in five key points:

1.   Take life seriously but with a pitch of salt (and humour)
2.   Don't buy battery farm eggs (and perhaps not Primark jeans either)
3.   Get a dog and a PhD, no matter how old you are (but only if you like dogs and PhDs)
4.   Don't ask anyone to do sex talk in German
5.   Come to my next comedy show

If you took away other five points, feel free to add your own personal conclusion here:

1.   _____
2.   _____
3.   _____
4.   _____
5.   Go to Alice's next comedy show

There may not be a God, but Louise Hay will always love you. And, I'm happy to confirm, not all handstands are bad handstands – you can have a lot of fun with women who wear rainbow-coloured shoelaces.

Thank you for buying this book. Please buy it for other people as well.

About the author

Alice Frick is an Austrian-born writer and comedian. She has written a lot of different material: comedy shows, books, screenplays and Christmas cards. Some of her work is published. Some isn't. She also has a website and a YouTube channel. Alice currently lives with her new computer in London. She can be found on stage in Central  London once a month hosting her regular comedy night featuring female comedians called 'Laughing Labia'.

Selected previous writing work by Alice:

A Frickin' Crazy Year (Solo show)
What the Frick (Sitcom)
Shop of Little Pleasures (Feature film)
Sketch me... if you can (Sketch series)
Hollywood, half of the whole truth (Unpublished book in German)
Your own enemy (Unpublished sad book in German)
Joke (Solo show)
Lesson Learned (Solo show)
Alles liebe Oma, 1992 (Christmas card)

Pink Zebra

PUBLISHING

Made in the USA
Columbia, SC
30 October 2023